{creativity}

{also by matthew fox}

The Coming of the Cosmic Christ:
The Healing of Mother Earth and the Birth of a Global Renaissance

Confessions: The Making of a Post-Denominational Priest

Creation Spirituality: Liberating Gifts for the Peoples of the Earth

Hildegard of Bingen's Book of Divine Works with Letters and Songs (editor)

Illuminations of Hildegard of Bingen

In the Beginning There Was Joy

Manifesto for a Global Civilization (with Brian Swimme)

Meditations with Meister Eckhart

Natural Grace: Dialogues on Creation, Darkness, and the Soul
in Spirituality and Science (with Rupert Sheldrake)

One River, Many Wells: Wisdom Springing from Global Faiths

Original Blessing: A Primer in Creation Spirituality

Passion for Creation: The Earth-Honoring Spirituality
of Meister Eckhart (formerly *Breakthrough*)

Prayer: A Radical Response to Life
(formerly *On Becoming a Musical, Mystical Bear*)

*The Physics of Angels: Exploring the Realm Where Science
and Spirit Meet* (with Rupert Sheldrake)

The Reinvention of Work: A New Vision of Livelihood for Our Time

Religion USA: Religion and Culture by Way of Time *Magazine*

Sheer Joy: Conversations with Thomas Aquinas on Creation Spirituality

*Sins of the Spirit, Blessings of the Flesh: Lessons for
Transforming Evil in Soul and Society*

*A Spirituality Named Compassion: Uniting Mystical
Awareness with Social Justice*

Western Spirituality: Historical Roots, Ecumenical Routes (editor)

*Whee! We, Wee All the Way Home: A Guide to
a Sensual, Prophetic Spirituality*

*Wrestling with the Prophets: Essays on Creation
Spirituality and Everyday Life*

WHERE THE DIVINE

{creativity}

AND THE HUMAN MEET

matthew fox

JEREMY P. TARCHER · PUTNAM
A MEMBER OF PENGUIN PUTNAM INC.
NEW YORK

Permissions are listed on page 245.

Most Tarcher/Putnam books are available at special quantity discounts for bulk purchase for sales promotions, premiums, fund-raising, and educational needs. Special books or book excerpts also can be created to fit specific needs. For details, write Putnam Special Markets, 375 Hudson Street, New York, NY 10014.

Jeremy P. Tarcher/Putnam
a member of
Penguin Putnam Inc.
375 Hudson Street
New York, NY 10014
www.penguinputnam.com

Library of Congress Cataloging-in-Publication Data

Fox, Matthew, date.
Creativity : where the divine and the human meet / Matthew Fox.
p.   cm.
Includes index.
ISBN 1-58542-178-2
1. Creative ability—Religious aspects—Christianity.   I. Title.
BT709.5.F69   2002   2002025697
291.2'2—dc21

Printed in the United States of America
1   3   5   7   9   10   8   6   4   2

This book is printed on acid-free paper. ∞

Book design by Jennifer Ann Daddio

This book is dedicated to the countless artists in my life, living and dead, students and teachers, musicians, poets, painters, playwrights, and more who make life come alive for me and all of us.

THANK YOU ALL!

{contents}

creative spirit, holy spirit

This book arose from a request from my publisher who heard me speak on the subject of "The Divine Artist Within" at the Unity Church of New York in New York City in June 2000. Some thoughts offered here also developed from a talk I was invited to give at the Art Institute of Chicago in 1993. I am grateful for the invitation to expand these talks, for in the process of writing this book I feel I have deepened my love and understanding of creativity.

I do not know any area of human potential more important if we are to be a sustainable species again. Creativity, when all is said and done, may be the best thing our species has going for it. It is also the most dangerous. I explore creativity here in the following manner: First I ask: How essential is creativity to our human nature? Chapters I and 2 explore this question: chapter 1 by exposing pseudo-meanings of being human, chapter 2 by proposing that creativity *is* our real nature. Creativity constitutes the very meaning of being human, and our powers of creativity distinguish us from other species. Evil, as well as profound goodness, transpires through our creativity.

Chapter 3 poses the question: "Where does creativity comes from?" Chapter 4 speaks of the Divine imagination that takes us into our creativity, as mystics have always taught and recognized. Chapter 5 considers two myths about creativity and its consequences: the Prometheus-Hercules myth and the Adam–Jesus Christ myth. Chapter 6 considers the obstacles to creativity that must be removed for creativity to flow—what is holding us back? Chapter 7 asks how we can tap more fully into our creative power, and chapter 8 speaks to cultural benefits that will flow when we bring creativity to bear on education, everyday life and relationships, politics and worship. Creativity assists us to move as a species to our next level of evolution.

When we consider creativity, we are considering the most elemental and innermost and deeply spiritual aspects of our beings. The great thirteenth-century mystic Meister Eckhart asks: "What is it that remains?" And his answer is: "That which is inborn in me remains." That which we give birth to from our depths is that which lives on after us. That which is inborn in us constitutes our most intimate moments—intimate with self, intimate with God the Creative Spirit, and intimate with others. To speak of creativity is to speak of profound intimacy. It is also to speak of our connecting to the Divine in us and of our bringing the Divine back to the community.

This is true whether we understand our creativity to be begetting and nourishing our children, making music, doing theater, gardening, writing, teaching, running a business, painting, constructing houses, or sharing the healing arts of medicine and therapy. Imagination brings about not just intimacy but a *big intimacy*, a sense of union with the cosmos, a sense of belonging and being at home, of our knowing we have not only a right to be here but a task to do as well while we are here. French philosopher Gaston Bachelard says that "great dreamers possess intimacy with the world." The artist in us and among us shares intimacy and returns one's intimacy to the world, nourishing the community with one's inner experience. This process of intimacy shared feels a lot like a sacred experience.

An example of what I mean can be found in a letter the psychologist Carl Rogers wrote about his work to theologian Paul Tillich. Rogers was very "secular" in his outlook until very near the end of his life, yet in this letter he confesses as follows: "I feel as though I am somehow in tune with the forces of the universe or that forces are operating through me in regard to this helping relationship." And his creativity as a therapist elicited awe from him: "I stand by with awe at the emergence of a self, a person, as I see a birth process in which I have had an important and facilitating part struggling to be himself, yet deathly afraid of being himself." I do not believe that Carl Rogers at work is that different from any of us in our work and relationships. In our creativity, however it is expressed, we can all feel "in tune with the forces of the universe," and the result of our work often urges us to "stand by with awe." Indeed, we must feel these things if we are to carry on with integrity.

The title of this book, *Creativity: Where the Divine and the Human Meet*, suggests that there is a special encounter with the Divine where creativity occurs. Is any place more intimate than the place where we create? Where we co-create with the Spirit of God and the Spirit of largesse that inspires our souls where we love? Where we make love? Where we love others through serving them with our labor? Where we love our children? Where we paint our truth? Where we dance our dance? Where we speak our words? Where we work? Where we utter our poetry?

The "our" is so big, so immense when we do these things. The "our" includes the hydrogen atoms of our bodies that are fourteen billion years old; the carbon and other atoms in us that are five billion years old; the food we have eaten and the drink we have drunk that give us the energy to work; the ideas that have penetrated our minds and impregnated our imaginations; the language we learned to speak so many years ago; the beauty and the pain we have absorbed through our days on earth.

Creativity is *intimate* because it is us most truly, spontaneously, and totally. It is also intimate because it is Spirit working through us in so profound a way that Eckhart says

God "becomes the space where" we want to act. Creativity is not a noun or even a verb—it is a place, a space, a gathering, a union, a *where*—wherein the Divine powers of creativity and the human power of imagination join forces. Where the two come together is where beauty and grace happen and, indeed, explode. Creativity constitutes the ultimate in intimacy, for it is the place where the Divine and the human are most destined to interact.

The word "where" contains its own sense of the infinite as well as the intimate. We speak of "somewhere" and "everywhere," of "nowhere" and "anywhere," of "elsewhere" and "wherever." The word "where" offers an invitation to the imagination to stretch to extremes of nothingness and everythingness . . . and beyond.

We might say that Divine intimacy is experienced as creativity and New Creation, which is accompanied by risk, surprise, and the courage needed for both. New Creation brings renewal, resurrection, and forgiveness with it. Creativity as Divine intimacy flows through us and is bigger than we are, urging us to go to the edge and grow larger. And our growth in turn delights God. "God is delighted to watch your soul enlarge," says Eckhart.

I began this book by intending to write on creativity but—as so often happens when the Spirit of Creativity has its way with us—something more was born. An insight about a theology of sin and grace emerged as I came to realize, during the course of its composition, that something else lay behind a recovery of a spirituality of creativity. To my surprise, I found myself writing a chapter on the meaning of Original Sin and Redemption, of Easter, Grace, and a theology of the Holy Spirit. Prometheus, Hercules, Christ, and Sophia were showing up. And yes, the historical Jesus as well. I propose that we do inherit an original wound, and that wound is directly related to the ambiguity of our very creative brains: Will we use our creativity to destroy or to bless with? Original sin means the repression of creativity, and redemption ought to be understood as *liberation from our fear of creativity.* Salvation is *the return of creativity,* which is the return of the Spirit. And Jesus (among others) died teaching and living these things. Easter becomes the resurrection of creativity itself and the overcoming of the fear of death that interferes with creativity. Pentecost becomes the sending of the Spirit of Creativity, which is the Holy Spirit.

I probably should not have been as surprised as I was, for if speaking of creativity constitutes speaking of our true, God-like, nature, it would stand to reason that the great stories of our history would address issues of creativity in their mysterious and mythical fashion. Why wouldn't a discussion of creativity unleash stories of guilt, fear of death, envy, sin, redemption, and grace? Why wouldn't creativity challenge the Divine itself, causing it to be threatened and even envious, as the Prometheus story tells us?

The great African-American mystic Howard Thurman once wrote that Christianity has "betrayed Jesus." Philosopher Thomas Sheehan writes of how "the Kingdom of God became Christianity," and scientist Peter Russell talks of "truth decay." There has been much "truth decay" in the church's imperial (Constantinian) ambitions that gave birth to agendas on original sin and redemption and "the only Son of God," all of which wandered far from the message of the historical Jesus. To say nothing of the church's often loud silence about our powers of creativity and imagination and its condemnations of the same.

Chaos reigns in our world today. Indigenous peoples and ancient forests are being exterminated along with an estimated thirty thousand species per year. Gaps are widening between the haves and have-nots of the world. Economies are faltering the world over. AIDS is spreading voraciously, especially in Africa, where entire nations are being swallowed up by a disease that is wasting one out of three persons. Transnational companies are exporting American capitalism and its value system to cultures that are thousands of years old and that succumb quickly to fast-food outlets and media invasions of Hollywood cinema and television sitcoms. Events at the World Trade Center, where thousands of people died in a vicious attack, remind us of our species' vast capacity for evil and hate and negative use of creativity. As do threats of bioterrorism.

What do we do with chaos? Creativity has an answer. We are told by those who have studied the processes of nature that creativity happens at the border between chaos and order. Chaos is a prelude to creativity. We need to learn, as every artist needs to learn, to live with chaos and, indeed, to dance with it as we listen to it and attempt some ordering.

Artists wrestle with chaos, take it apart, deconstruct *and* reconstruct from it. Accept the challenge to convert chaos into some kind of order, respecting the timing of it all, not pushing beyond what is possible—combining holy patience *with* holy impatience: That is the role of the artist. It is each of our roles as we launch the twenty-first century, because we are all called to be artists in our own way. We were all artists as children. We need to study the chaos around us in order to turn it into something beautiful. Something sustainable. Something that remains.

African-American philosopher bell hooks talks about the need for an *aesthetic revolution* and proposes that our times offer an opportunity either where ties will be severed or "new and varied forms of bonding" can occur. We can make new and unheard-of connections between classes and differing races and cultures by way of the aesthetic. How is this possible? Because the poorest of the poor are "thinking about aesthetics." hooks says: "On the terrain of culture, one can participate in critical dialogue with the uneducated poor, the black underclass who are thinking about aesthetics." She finds great hope and energy in this possibility of engaging different classes and ethnic groups around aesthetics. "It's exciting to think, write, talk about and create art that reflects passionate engagement with popular culture, because this may very well be 'the' central future location of resistance struggle, a meeting place where new and radical happenings can occur." hooks is advocating putting imagination to the use of transformation.

I concur. I do not see any way out of humankind's multiple dilemmas except that one route that got us here the first place: our powerful creativity. But how to apply our creativity *at the service of justice and compassion* is the lesson taught by all spiritual traditions, and it is a lesson of survival for our times. As the Dalai Lama has put it: "We can reject everything else: religion, ideology, all received wisdom. But we cannot escape the necessity of love and compassion."

To allow creativity its appropriate place in our lives and our culture, our education and our family relationships, is to allow healing to happen at a profound level. The intimacy of creativity corresponds to the mystical experience itself. Mysticism bespeaks union, and there is an ongoing union of us and the Divine precisely during the process of giving birth in any form whatsoever. We lose track of time and of place, we move into a timeless time and a placeless space when we are in a creative state. Afterward, we know we have tasted something worth remembering, something that will last. And often we have a special gift to bestow on others because of the journey we have undergone in our creative work.

A French philosopher once commented on the work of painter Lapicque in the following manner: He "demands of the creative act that it should offer him as much surprise as life itself." Our creativity is meant to surprise—just as life does. Furthermore, art means "an increase of life, a sort of competition of surprises that stimulates our consciousness and keeps it from becoming somnolent."

The alternatives to creativity put to the use of intimacy,

surprise, and compassion are not only to wallow in passivity or luxury living and cynicism, while the earth burns all around us à la Nero on a planetary scale, but also to turn our Divine powers of creativity over to demonic uses. This is strong language—Divine/demonic—but it is necessary language for stating the truth of things. The truth is that our creativity is so powerful, so without precedent in the history of evolution, that it is literally taking over the planet. Scientists now tell us that evolution has been supplanted on this planet by culture. Human culture moves at so rapid a pace that it has far outrun and outstripped the natural processes of change and adaptation.

This means we are already playing God whether we want to or not, whether we admit it or not. We have taken over the processes of evolution on this planet. How are we doing? Not very well from the looks of things.

No one can consider twentieth-century history and not see the demonic in human creativity that was birthed in that era: the first and second world wars with their wiping out of civilian populations on an unprecedented scale; the making of the first atomic weapon ("now we know evil," spoke Oppenheimer, the father of that project); the amassing of nuclear weapons and delivery systems; the invention of gas ovens to more efficiently exterminate an entire race of humans; the genocide in Cambodia under Pol Pot; in Rwanda; in Stalin's Russia; the gradual warming of the planet as we dump more and more carbon dioxide into the atmosphere, oblivious of its consequences for other species and other generations; the fouling of our rivers, oceans, fisheries, ozone protection, forests, and soil; and terrorism in the name of fundamentalist religion. All these actions took creativity. They all took imagination. They were misuses of our imaginations. Can we learn the lesson of that? Can we come to grips with our Divine/demonic power in this century?

We must. We have no other choice. Whether our species is sustainable or not depends on our wrestling creativity back from the brink of its demonic potential. To move our Divine powers of creativity from serving the demonic to serving the Divine is to move from art for art's sake and art for advertising's sake and art for power's sake to art for compassion's sake. Art for the sake of planetary health and well-being. Art for celebration's sake. Art for building bridges' sake. This constitutes an aesthetic revolution, which is a nonviolent revolution.

In this book I reconstruct Christianity and culture around the number-one survival issue of our time: the sustainability achieved when creativity is honored and practiced not for its own sake but for justice and compassion's sake. *This* is the way of the Holy Spirit, who *is* the Spirit of Creativity and compassion. And who *was present* hovering over the waters at the beginning of creation and *is present* still at the continuance of creation (Aboriginals call this the "Dreamtime") and who *is present* in the mind of the artist at work— which is each of us; And whose presence melts the Tower of Babel, that is, the divisions between cultures, religions, and peoples.

Hildegard of Bingen taught about this Spirit in the following manner:

Who is the Holy Spirit? The Holy Spirit is a Burning Spirit. It kindles the hearts of humankind. Like tympanum and lyre it plays them, gathering volume in the temple of the soul. . . .
The Holy Spirit is the life of the life of all creatures . . . that gives existence to all form. . . .
The Holy Spirit resurrects and awakens everything that is.

May our species be resurrected and awakened by the Spirit of Creativity for this coming century. May we be ennobled to carry on the next stage of our evolution. May this book make a modest contribution to that effort.

October 4, 2001
UNIVERSITY OF CREATION SPIRITUALITY
NAROPA OAKLAND
OAKLAND, CALIFORNIA

who are we as a species?

 Our planet, so under the control of and almost at the mercy of humans, finds itself at a crossroads. It is a time for getting to the essence of things, for withdrawing from the deluge of distractions that so often make up our existence. It is time to ask the basic questions again:

- Who are we?
- Why are we here?
- How are we doing?
- Is the path we are on as a species a healthy one for ourselves, our planet, and our children's children's children's children to come?
- If our path is not a healthy one, what are we doing about it? What can we do about it?

- What constitutes our authentic strength as a species?
- What constitutes our gravest dangers as a species?

I wish to explore these questions in the chapters that follow. I will be as direct as I can be. We are all too busy to beat around the bush on matters as important as those that face us today—issues of our collective extinction as a species and issues that raise the awesome questions of the ongoing extinction of species other than our own. Scientific observers tell us that we are going through the *greatest extinction spasm in the last sixty-five million years of this planet.* That is amazing. It is scary. And, above all, it is us!

Our species and its technological culture are more responsible for this extinction spasm than any other single cause. It is our wastes, our release of carbon dioxide through automobiles and fossil fuels, that are warming the planet, causing the end of species like the polar bear whose young cannot grow to maturity on ice floes any longer because the ice floes are melting too rapidly. It is our factories and cattle farms that are poisoning rivers, soil, forests, and air, and thereby bringing about so much death. Ours has become a necrophiliac civilization. We have become death-bringers. Was it always this way? Was that why we were brought into existence? What can we do about this sad situation?

Let us begin by addressing the age-old question: Who are we? by first looking at who we are not.

WHO WE ARE NOT

Judging from the trouble our species causes one another and the planet, it would seem we don't know ourselves awfully well. A good way to approach a serious effort at self-understanding is to first treat the negative (the via negativa). If we are not sure of who we are, we might at least begin with *who we are not*. This is an especially important methodology to enact when we live in a culture whose media and advertisers and users of the media, such as politicians, corporations, and sports entertainers, are constantly busy telling us who *they think* we are or ought to be. By naming who we are not, we are circling around to explore who we are, and we are clarifying and distinguishing our reality from those who would foist a particular version of reality upon us. We are undergoing a process of clarification that can lead up to a working definition of who we really are.

1. We Are Not Consumers

For the vast majority of our time on earth, our species did not buy its food or its clothing or its shelter or its education or its medical healing. We chased down our food, skinned rabbits and deer and buffalo for clothing, found caves and built shelters of buffalo hides attached to tree trunks, and carved limbs and even buffalo bones, and sought out plants that heal. Our elders told the important stories around campfires, healers studied plants for their powers and chanted to the heavens for theirs. In short, for 98 percent of our existence as hunter-gatherers, we did not consume. We created. Ten thousand years ago, in a creative discovery that has proven to be a mixed blessing indeed, we started to plant things. We no longer imitated the prairie in the way it seeded itself patiently each year: We hurried the process along and chose to do our own planting. We called this "agriculture." Agriculture was not a moment of "pure progress" for humankind. It looked like a good deal—we could choose our diets no matter what the game were doing in our neighborhoods; we could stay home more and wander less; we could even have some people do the seeding and growing while others gathered in villages and then cities and were fed by the growers. But we paid a great price for this.

Wes Jackson of the Land Institute feels that we have been doing farming wrong for ten thousand years. The mistakes made ten thousand years ago have become much more exaggerated in recent times with the addition of technological breakthroughs. The soil has suffered terribly. With sowing and harvesting come erosion. There is only so much soil. As our population expanded and even exploded, the food needs were so pressing that we did almost anything to get more food from the soil: pesticides, fertilizers, machinery, agribusiness—all this has developed to satisfy the consumer. It has rendered the consumer often passive and uncreative at growing the food we need and quite oblivious to where food comes from. It has taught us to take food for granted. Those who have the money to buy it, that is. And those who don't? Those who do not qualify as consumers, because they cannot buy or charge to credit cards, are very often left without food and the other basics. The world is divided between the consumers and the nonconsumers, who are being inducted into being wanna-be consumers.

A similar story could be told about the clothes on our backs (and those that stuff and fill our overflowing closets). There was a time when we made our clothes—chased down the skins and hides and later grew the cotton or harvested the silk and sewed and stitched and wove and wove.

Are we here to be consumers? Is consuming the essence of who we are? It would seem not. For most of our existence we were makers, not consumers; we were hunters and gatherers, not consumers. We made our clothes, shelter, and education.

2. We Are Not Addicts

Addiction is everywhere in our culture. Addiction is about habits that take us over, that "dictate" (the same word as "addiction") to us what we ought to be eating or doing or relating to. The very nature of much of our advertising industry is to render us addictive. Much of our most highly advertised products, such as cigarettes, Coca-Cola, Pepsi, cereals, coffee, etc., contain ingredients that are addictive, such as nicotine, cocaine (Coca-Cola and coffee), sugar (Coca-Cola and other soft drinks and many cereals). Fats (as in potato chips) and salt—that our palates find appealing—are addictive-forming. Powerful forces are making huge profits by getting us addicted. Of course there is also alcohol and its addictive-forming possibilities. And drugs. And sex. And work. And co-dependent relationships. And religion. And money. And power.

We are a species and indeed a civilization very prone to dictatorships, that is, to addiction. It is as if we want to turn our power over to others. To lay back and let others have power over us. The thirteenth-century theologian Thomas Aquinas defined "greed" as a "quest for the infinite." Is a quest for the infinite not behind every addiction? Isn't addiction, by definition, never having enough? Always wanting another hit? Does greed play a profound role in every addiction? Do greed and addiction take us over as individuals and as a society at the same time?

I propose that most addictions come from our surrendering our own real powers, that is, our powers of creativity. We get a temporary "high" from a shot of some external stimulus, be it nicotine or sugar, speed or acid, sex or more money, entertainment or television—and that is our sad substitute for the joy and ecstasy of creativity and creation. If we were creative, would we be so addicted? If we are addicted, can we be creative? Creativity may be the authentic experience of the infinite. If that is so—and we will explore this more later in this book—then creativity would seem to be the medicine for addiction. Creativity, unlike addiction which is always an external referent, is an interior one. It comes from the inside out. It comes from a very different place than does addiction. An *addictive society* does not encourage creativity and is, in fact, terrified of it. Instead of creativity, couchpotatoitis.

3. We Are Not Passive Couch Potatoes

It is not the essence of the human to be passive. We are players. We are actors on many stages. We initiate contacts, ideas, movements, inventions, babies, institutions, sport, exercise, relationships of all kinds. We are curious, we are yearning to wonder, we are longing to be amazed, we are eager to grow, to learn, to be excited, to be enthusiastic, to be expressive. In short, to be *alive*.

Passivity is a sign of sickness, of weakness, of dying. That time will come for all of us. Why hasten the moment? Why not live fully first? Why surrender to others our sacred time, our sacred powers, to act and express ourselves? My own experience is that when I am depressed, I want to watch television. Television occupies my mind, cutting it off from problems that beset me. That is one of its seductive accomplishments. Of course, at its best, television can occasionally educate us, inform us, refresh us, and even gather us as a community. A good example of the latter is the gathering of artists who donated their music to heal the nation after the devastating blow to New York City when the WTC was attacked.

But television addiction is invariably vicarious living or it is helping us to numb some pain in our daily lives. We do not have to become couch potatoes when we watch TV.

That happens as part of the addictive process. We can *choose* not to be addicted to TV. We can choose to create ourselves without it, to spend our leisure time doing other things—riding a bike, hiking, running, reading, listening to music, dancing, conversing, writing poetry, painting, meditating, gardening, learning. Creativity may be the opposite of couchpotatoitis.

4. We Are Not Boring

To be boring is to be uninteresting. We are not an uninteresting species. Indeed, the more we learn of our history, the more interesting we become to ourselves. To be among indigenous peoples as they make preparations for a powwow or a sundance, for a sweat lodge or a communal meal, is anything but uninteresting. The costumes, the headdresses, the music, the drum, the songs sung and chanted, the foods gathered and cooked, the teaching that goes on with the young and not so young, the adjustments when it is raining, when hot rocks for the sweat lodges grow cold, when heat overtakes the participants—what is boring about any of that?

Our music, our art, our dance, our theater, our ritual, our love-making—what is boring about that? The architecture in our cities, the awesome buildings that defy gravity, the bridges that connect cities as they span the waters, the traffic patterns that amazingly work so that everyone finds their way home at night, the sewers and water lines and gas lines underneath our cities, the wildness of the myriad of peoples walking in the city streets, all with their places to go to or from, the churches and mosques and synagogues that depict our yearning for Spirit and a wholeness we feel estranged from, the good works of people dedicated to the sick, the hungry, the dying, the forgotten, the lonely, the imprisoned—we are not a boring species. Say what you will.

Even our wars, our planning for wars, our sick desire to take war to the heavens and call it defense—even our capacity for folly and for self-delusion—are evidences that we are not boring. Our crimes, our devastation of beautiful and healthy habitats for other species to live in and who provide our minds with wonder and beauty—even our crimes are evidence that we are not a boring species. Dangerous? Yes. Boring? No.

5. We Need Not Be Bored

A boring or uninteresting people are a bored people. But people who are interesting and do interesting things and give birth to interesting realities are not bored. If we are alive and interacting with all the marvel of daily existence, if we are learning how others, living and deceased, related to the marvel of existence, then we will not be bored. We will not be reduced to a state of disequilibrium or depression wherein we cannot move, wherein we have no energy to "begin new things" (Thomas Aquinas's definition of "acedia," the capital sin of boredom or sloth or ennui at living).

As we learn more about our story as a species and how we came to be over a fourteen-billion-year period of amazing goings-on in the universe, we realize how unboring and how very special existence is. We get renewed and awakened and amazed and alert to ask: What can I contribute? What did the universe have in mind in spending fourteen billion years of work to bring me and the likes of me to be here?

At these times we are asking truths about who we are and what our purpose is for being here. We are no longer taking our existence for granted—nor are we taking our ancestors for granted. These ancestors, we are learning, include the original fireball, the hydrogen and helium atoms that it gave birth to, the galaxies that birthed the supernovas that birthed the stars that birthed the earth that birthed the waters and the continents and the plants and the animals and the ozone and the sun and the moon and the seeds and the trees and flowers—all of which were necessary for our presence to occur.

No one who lives in our world and is at all aware of where we come from can ever be bored—or boring—again. Being awake is the opposite of being bored. Or boring. Buddha's name means "the awakened one." He and countless other spiritual figures invite us to come awake. To resist boredom. To resist taking for granted.

6. We Are Not Cogs in a Machine

The modern era that has dominated our civilization for the past three hundred years, and which has in great part taken over the planet with its inventions and its ideas, left us with the notion that the universe is a machine, that our bodies are machines, that the earth and sky are machines. If God existed, God was a tender of the machine, the man with the oil can to keep the machinery of the universe running.

But if we live in a machine, then we are mere cogs in it, mere pieces that just happened to show up. Our main duty is to shut up and obey—obey the economic machine, the political machine, the military machine, the religious machine, the educational machine. To live inside a machine is scary business. Fear takes over. Anxiety increases. Numbness multiplies. Meaninglessness becomes more widespread than meaning. Coldness dominates. Sterility reigns. Creativity dies. Passivity becomes a virtue.

Machines are cold and very large. They have an agenda all their own. We can only shrink our souls down and learn to obey and get out of its way. Creativity gets stifled. It must be discouraged. Who wants to upset the machine? To get it angry? Or even to get noticed by it? We want to get out of its way, shrink from its attention, hide in a corner, look for its benign side. Living in a machine universe may be the ultimate expression of a dysfunctional relationship. There is no mutuality there.

Maybe this is why dysfunctional relationships have so swollen in numbers during this industrial age from which we are emerging with our souls barely intact. Indeed, emerging with not having a clue what "soul" even means anymore. Emerging but having lost so many of our relationships with the beauty and power of species all around us. Emerging lonely and lost, disempowered and depressed, sad and set up for an infinite variety of addictions. But emerging all the same, because somehow inside all of us, and in spite of toxic teachings we have inherited, there lies deep within a creative force that wants to give life and taste life in abundance.

7. *We Are Not Lazy*

Our species is not lazy. We are not without energy. It only seems that we are at times. But this is because of "acedia," it is because we get taken over by forces that strip us of our excitement and our appreciation for living. Rabbi Abraham Joshua Heschel says that humankind will perish not from lack of information but from lack of appreciation. How right he is! When gratitude reigns, energy reigns. When thankfulness is real, praise happens. Praise is never lazy. Praise extends itself, sacrifices, gives away. Praise is effusive; it goes out to others.

At the heart of all creativity there lies praise, there lies a hidden "thank you," a yearning to return blessing for blessing. This is how the great psychologist Otto Rank defines the artist: "one who wants to leave behind a gift." Why would one be intent on leaving a gift behind if one had not intuited that life, for all of its woe and troubles, is essentially praiseworthy and deserving of our gratitude?

Gratitude is the ultimate enabler. Gratitude moves us from apparent laziness to heroic giving. Never underestimate the power of gratitude. It can move mountains. It can build great things. It can arouse us to action. That is why gratitude is the ultimate prayer, as Meister Eckhart tells us when he says: "If the only prayer you say in your whole life is 'thank you,' that would suffice." It suffices to get us moving, get us giving birth, get us creating.

8. We Are Not Destroyers

Finally, it must be said that, while humankind does destroy, it is not of our essence to do so. We often choose to destroy, but destruction is a *choice.*

The essence of our nature is to give birth, not to destroy. To create. We see this in the love of mother and child and in the love of artist for his or her art. The dilemma is that the very powers we possess for creativity can just as easily become employed to destroy with. Consider the twentieth-century's preoccupation with weaponry and war. From nuclear warheads to nuclear submarines to carry them, from gas in the wartime trenches to gas ovens—we have used our amazing imaginations to imagine how to kill more efficiently. Consider the chemicals we have invented that are seeping into soil and waters everywhere and that have not been tested for their destructive aftereffects. I do not observe that any other animals we know of are destroyers. They may kill another species, but they do not destroy whole habitats of other species. There seems to be a balance in the rest of nature that gets out of control with humans. Why is this so?

The answer, I am convinced, has to do with what is most unique in our species. It is our powerful, almost God-like, imaginations. It is our creativity itself that lies at the essence of our humanity. This creativity is so powerful that with it we can create or destroy. Like the Scriptures say: "I put before you life and death. Choose life." What is before us is the power of creativity—it is a life-and-death power. What is also before us is choice: It is a daily choice, an everyday choice, one that arises in all our relations from parenting to grandparenting, from work worlds to educational ones, from religion to economics, business, politics, and citizenship in all its forms. It affects what we eat and what we throw away; how we live and what we choose to say no to. This is the power of creativity. "Creativity" may be the nearest one-word definition we possess for the essence of our humanity, for the true meaning of "soul."

creativity,
our true nature

In caves in Africa, high above the shores of the Indian Ocean, scientists have recently discovered artifacts dating to seventy-seven thousand years ago. These findings indicate that human culture as we know it began in Africa, not in Europe; and it began about forty thousand years earlier than we had previously figured. Anatomically modern humans began in Africa at least one hundred thirty thousand years ago, but it is by their artifacts and art work that archaeologists determine how human these beings were. It is of our very nature to make artifacts. It is of our very nature to create.

St. Paul writes about knowing our "true nature." That is what we are trying to articulate here. Having examined our false nature above, our illusory or mistaken ideas of our nature, we can ask: Who are we truly?

I propose that when all is said and done, *our true nature is our creativity.* Psychologist Rollo May concurs when he says: "The creative process must be explored not as the product of sickness, but as representing the highest degree of emotional health, as the expression of the normal people in the act of actualization of themselves."

When the Bible declares that we are made in the "image and likeness" of the Creator, it is affirming that creativity is at our core just as it lies at the core of the Creator of all things. Not only the Bible but other traditions also celebrate our nearness to the creative powers of Divinity. The Sufi mystic Hafiz declares:

> *All the talents of God are within you.*
> *How could this be otherwise*
> *When your soul*
> *derived from His genes!*

An ancient Mesoamerican poet tells us that God dwells in the heart of the artist and the artist draws God out of his or her heart when the artist is at work.

We are creators at our very core. Only creating can make us happy, for in creating we tap into the deepest powers of self and universe and the Divine Self. We become co-creators, that is, we create *with* the other forces of society, universe, and the Godself when we commit to creativity.

But what is creativity? We might begin with what we learned from the previous chapter. Going through the list of names for our *illusory* natures, we might understand creativity, our true nature, as being the opposite. Who are we then? We are makers and fabricators, we are free, we are active, we are interesting, we are interested and curious, we are part of a vast creative universe, we are energetic and alive, we are creators and co-creators.

Scholars of evolutionary history are telling us that today biological evolution is being overwhelmed by cultural evolution. The human species, which evolves by culture more than by slow-moving biological change, is overwhelming the planet. All the more reason to examine that element that makes human culture so amazingly rich and fast-moving: human creativity.

British scientist Peter Russell comments on how profoundly human culture is overwhelming biological evolution. "Our mind and hands represent a new source of 'newness,' putting at Nature's disposal a fundamentally new mechanism of evolution." What now most affects our development is no longer "our genes but our ideas." With ideas and the creativity to put them into action, we can turn space into a home away from home, we can turn places of 120-degree heat into dwelling places through air conditioning, we can live under the sea for months at a time, we can turn arctic places into cozy, insulated homes. This means we are speeding up evolution profoundly, since it would take thousands of years for biological changes in our skin or metabolism to adapt to such diverse climates.

Russell goes on to say that our technological creations

"are also part of evolution. . . . Now, with the appearance of *Homo sapiens,* a new form of evolution has become possible. It is our minds and hands that are doing the molding, reorganizing matter into new structures and creating new capacities." Human creativity is affecting evolution like never before. We are integral to it, we are speeding it up on this planet, we are a force to be reckoned with—for good or for ill. "Mind has now become the dominant creative force on this planet," Russell warns us and he offers examples such as the following:

- The solar cell, by converting the sun's energy directly into electricity, "represents a totally new method of capturing the sun's energy." He sees this "as significant a breakthrough as the development of photosynthesis itself, some three billion years ago."
- "Radar allows us to 'see' new ranges of frequencies— a development as significant as the evolution of the eye."
- Through nuclear physics we discover how to create new chemical compounds. The last time this happened was with the supernova explosion over five billion years ago.

If it is true that "mind has now become the dominant creative force on this planet," then it is more important than ever to examine our powers of creativity and learn to discipline them.

Scientist Brian Swimme uses the following story to remind us of how ancient and how necessary for survival is our creativity. When our ancestors discovered fire back in the savannahs of Africa over a million years ago, they set out on a great journey. When they arrived at the place we now call EuroAsia, the ice age broke out. There they were, fresh from the heat of Africa, forced to live in caves for seven hundred thousand years. Did they give up? Did they fall into masochism and say, "Woe is we!"? No. They got to work. They put their imaginations to work. They learned how to prepare hides, sew warm outfits, hunt animals for food and clothing, and how to tell tales around the campfire and entertain themselves. In short, this is where our creativity came to birth.

I draw two important lessons from this story. First is how strong our ancestors were. There are few adaptations that we are being asked to make today that are as profound as the adaptation from the heat of the African savannahs to the ice age. A second lesson I conclude is the realization of how *basic* our creativity is to our survival. Creativity and imagination are not frosting on a cake: They are integral to our sustainability. They are survival mechanisms. They are of the essence of who we are. They constitute our deepest empowerment.

Psychologist Otto Rank saw creativity as so basic to the essence of our humanness that he, in effect, substituted the human creative impulse or the drive for *production* for Freud's emphasis on sexuality and *reproduction*. As Rankian scholar Robert Kramer puts it: "It is only in the individual act of will [i.e., a choice to create] that we have the unique phenomenon of spontaneity, the establishing of a new primary cause." Because of our capacity for self-consciousness, "the human begins a new series of causes." We become causes of things and take on what Thomas Aquinas called the "dignity of causality" in a special way.

For Rank, at the heart of our dignity lies our power of creativity, where the human being "becomes at once creator and creature or actually moves from creature to creator, in the ideal case, creator of himself, his own personality." Our ultimate act of creativity is giving birth to who we are, and this individuality comes from a series of births corresponding to "a continued result of births, rebirths, and a new birth, which reach from the birth of the child from the mother, beyond the birth of the individual from the mass, to the birth of creative work from the individual and finally to the birth of knowledge from the work." Thus our whole life long we are involved in creativity of the profoundest kind—unless we opt out of this responsibility. And this opting out corresponds, in Rank's view, to neurosis itself.

Rank observes that while the individual is at once creator and creature, in neurosis "the creative expression of will is a negative one, resting on the denial of the creator role." Rank learned that a lot of emotional problems are creatively brought about by the neurotic in a process he called a "gain through illness," which derives from a "philosophy of suffering." This pain "is self-willed, a sort of creation that can find expression only in this negative, destructive way." Since neurosis is a negative act of creativity, healing can happen through redirecting one's creative impulses to love of life rather than love of suffering, to creativity rather than control. The neurotic has failed to achieve normal development and corresponds to the failed artist (artiste manqué). "Both illness and work are the expression of the creative will in the individual." The artiste manqué is one who has failed to accept the burden of his or her difference. Every responsible artist comes to grips with his or her differentiation from others. There follows an immense feeling of guilt for "unused life, the unlived in us," when we fail our responsibility to give birth as we are here to do.

It is because creativity is so central to our hearts and souls as human beings that Rank puts it at the same level as love itself as a sign of our health and well-being. Creativity and relationship, art and love, express our deepest beings, and what they share in common is empathy. "In the jointly created—and endlessly re-created—'moment' of empathy between artist and enjoyer, lover and beloved, I and Thou, client and therapist, separateness is dissolved only to be rediscovered, enriched and renewed by the dissolution of the individual into the void." Both love and art take us into the void and beyond in a kind of rhythm of birth and rebirth that never ceases. Rank compares this process to an encounter with the Divine: "For this very essence of man, his soul, which the artist puts into his work and which is represented by it, is found again in the work by the enjoyer just as the believer finds his soul in religion or in God with whom he feels himself to be one. It is on this identity of the spiritual . . . and not on a psychological identification with the artist that [aesthetic pleasure] ultimately depends." Art is a spiritual experience. And the misuse of art is a daimonic one.

In his book *Love and Will*, Rollo May, standing on Rank's shoulders, defines the daimonic this way: "The daimonic is the urge in every being to affirm itself, assert itself, perpetuate and increase itself . . . aggression, hostility, cruelty [are] the reverse side of the same assertion which empowers our creativity. All life is a flux between these two aspects of the daimonic. We can repress the daimonic, but we cannot avoid the toll of apathy and the tendency toward later explosion which such repression brings in its wake." May, like Rank, believes that we can choose to integrate the daimonic into our personality by freeing the constructive or positive will *or* we can bottle it up and expect, as he says, "explosions." He believes that when the daimonic urge is integrated into the personality "it results in creativity."

CREATIVITY AND THE DEMONIC:
EVIL AND CREATIVITY

To understand our individual neuroses as daimonic is one thing, but our species is capable of evil on a still larger scale, and this, too, results from our powerful potential for quasi-divine creativity. We can—and ought to—speak about our capacity for evil and destruction as approaching the *demonic.* Thomas Aquinas uttered a powerful reminder, a strong wake-up call, when he said seven centuries ago: "One human being can do more evil than all the other species put together." These words were uttered seven hundred years before Hitler or Stalin or Pol Pot existed.

What is behind them? What is being revealed to us here? What we are being told is that human creativity is no small thing; in fact, it is unique in the universe or at least in this corner of the universe we call earth. Our planet does not know other species that can accomplish nearly the destruction we can when we put our minds to it. Our capacity for dysfunction, for destruction, for malice, for evil is unparalleled among the creatures of the earth.

Why is this? It is because of our "fierce imaginations." Our powers for creativity can be used for blessing or for curse, for life or for death, for necrophilia or for biophilia. We do have choices. We can choose how to use our creativity and for what purposes. Another way of saying this is to say that our creativity is not only where the Divine and the human meet but also where the Divine and the demonic meet.

There are many examples to bear this out. Consider hydrogen weapons. Consider biological weapons. Consider the warming of the planet that industrial technology has brought about on a mass scale in about two hundred years. Consider the torture instruments of the Inquisition and the sadism it taps into. Consider economic systems and ideologies that make the rich richer and the poor poorer and that build on the worst instincts of human nature, such as greed and gluttony (of which today's word is "consumerism") and anthropocentrism. (One CEO of a logging company said that when he looks at a twenty-five-hundred-year-old tree he does not see a tree but "a pile of cash extending up to the sky.") Consider the sweatshops and child labor and slavery trades of the nineteenth century, as well as the sex trade of children and women that is taking place still today in the twenty-first century.

It is as if human imagination has no bounds when it comes to the uses it puts itself to. This is where justice and compassion must play a great role: to guide, steer, and bridle our imaginations so that they serve a greater cause. And it also underscores the stakes involved in waking up to our own, everyday creativity, for if we are not in touch with our powers of imagination and help to steer them in healthy directions, then we are surrendering our ethical decision making to others. And these others, be they individuals or corporations, have their own agendas, which may prove to be very distant from our own values and ethics.

In short, the capacity for evil in our species is so profound because our creativity is so deep. All the more reason to honor, explore, discipline, and steer our creative imaginations. Buddhist teacher Thich Nhat Hanh tells us that we are all born with seeds of violence and with seeds of peace in us but that we must water and nourish the seeds of peace if they are to grow. Furthermore, society itself has its own agenda—which is often biased in favor of seeds of violence—and so we have to work all the harder at the peace development. Peace, I would propose, is not the absence of war so much as the directing of our creativity to serve and bring about compassion. "Seeds of peace" are equivalent to seeds of creativity. But so, too, are "seeds of violence." Steering creativity into healthy directions is all of our responsibility.

Evil happens not just in our misuse and misdirection of our creativity. It also happens because of what tradition calls "sins of omission," that is, because of our failure to stretch our imaginations to the fullest. Poet Denise Levertov puts it well when she warns us that "man's capacity for evil, then, is less a positive capacity, for all its horrendous activity, than a failure to develop man's most human function, the imagination, to its fullness, and consequently a failure to develop compassion."

{three}

where does creativity come from?

If creativity is as close to the essence of our being human as we are saying, then an important question to ask is the following: Where does creativity come from? How old is it—how long has it been around? What are its origins? When we can address these questions, we might be able to address how best to tap into creativity, how best to discipline and utilize it. In this chapter, we will offer three answers to the question: "Where does creativity come from?" One answer does not exclude the others. All may be working together in harmony within us and around us.

1. Creativity Comes from the Universe Itself

I recently asked Dr. Apela Colorado, an Oneida woman and director of the program in Recovering the Indigenous Mind at Naropa University and the University of Creation Spirituality, this question: "Where do you think creativity comes from?" Her answer was as follows: "We greet the sun every morning—the sun's rising is where creativity begins. Look to the moon and the stars for guidance from above—all this contains the story of our creativity."

The fact that she immediately guided me to the universe for the origin of our human imagination and creativity is very wise. Creativity is not a human invention or a human power isolated from the other powers of the universe. Quite the opposite. First came the universe's power of creativity; only very lately did humans arrive on the scene with theirs. The modern view of the world did not endorse this notion of the omnipresence of creativity in the universe. The universe, as we have seen, was considered to be dead, inert, and machinelike. But the ancient peoples, the premoderns, never saw it that way. Neither does today's science.

Consider, for example, how the worship of the goddess was an honoring of the creative principle that permeated the universe and how this honoring undergirded a culture that was peace-oriented and not war-oriented. Marija Gimbutas reports that "the Goddess in all her manifestations was a symbol of the unity of all life in Nature. Her power was in water and stone, in tomb and cave, in animals and birds, snakes and fish, hills, trees, and flowers. Hence the holistic and mythopoeic perception of the sacredness and mystery of all there is on Earth." To honor creativity is to sow the seeds of peace in human hearts and in culture. Thomas

Berry believes that these early cultures identified "maternal nurturance as the primordial creating, sustaining, and fulfilling power of the universe. Mutual nurturance is presented as the primary bonding of each component of the universe with the other components. This experience of the universe as originating in and sustained by a primordial originating and nurturing principle imminent in the universe itself finds expression in the figure of the Goddess in the late Paleolithic Period and in the Neolithic Period in the New East.

"This goddess figure presided over this period as a world of meaning, of security, of creativity in all its forms. This was not a matriarchy, nor was it a social program. It was a comprehensive cosmology of a creative and nurturing principle independent of any associated male figure." The lesson learned in this period of human history was clear: Creativity derived from the goddess and was present throughout nature and found within things in an immanent way. It was found within humans as well as within the rest of nature.

Today's science is also instructing us in the origins of creativity and finding that the whole universe is permeated with the power of change and birth. Physicist Brian Swimme summarizes the findings of science in this way: "If you let hydrogen gas alone for 13 billion years it will become giraffes, rose bushes and humans." This is another way of saying that *everything* has within itself the power of creativity, the power of giving birth, the power of surprising us (and presumably itself as well). One might say that hydrogen gas has the goddess busy creating within it.

Just how prevalent are the powers of creativity in the universe according to today's science? Thomas Berry sees creativity as intrinsic to the very process of evolution. "The emergent process, as noted by the geneticist Theodore Dobzhansky, is neither random nor determined but creative. Just as in the human order, creativity is neither a rational deductive process nor the irrational wandering of the undisciplined mind but the emergence of beauty as mysterious as the blossoming of a field of daisies out of the dark Earth." Furthermore, the creativity of the evolutionary process "follows the general pattern of all creativity."

Sri Aurobindo believes that "the supreme creative stimulus" occurs in the great ages of literature worldwide when there is a "pouring of a new and greater self-vision of man and Nature and existence" into humanity, one that expands the human soul and mind. With a new creation story, a new "creative stimulus" has indeed arrived, one that can expand our souls and minds.

Berry recognizes that at the heart of the earth community there lies a creativity that is nothing short of wild. "The community itself and each of its members has ultimately a wild component, a creative spontaneity that is its deepest reality, its most profound mystery." This wildness is found in the human imagination as well. All artists undergo it. The quest for survival and the quest for food arise in creatures and elicit their wildness. Surely New York City, a human creation, is a wild habitat. Spirit is everywhere. One needs to be alert not to miss the action, and one needs to be able to withdraw and turn off the senses, too, in order to return with energy to the streets each day. Wisdom and compassion are not enemies. They are poles of a common axis. We need, the artist needs, both.

With spontaneity comes wildness—both emanate from deep within creatures. Berry comments: "Wildness we might consider as the root of the authentic spontaneities of any being. It is that wellspring of creativity whence comes the instinctive activities that enable all living beings to obtain their food, to find shelter, to bring forth their young: to sing and dance and fly through the air and swim through the depths of the sea. This is the same inner tendency that evokes the insight of the poet, the skill of the artist and the power of the shaman."

Berry believes that a tension exists between wildness and discipline and that we can see that tension, so necessary for creativity, playing itself out in the earth system itself. Among the planets we know, an excess of discipline suppressed the wildness of Mars and resulted in very little life there; the excess of wildness suppressed the discipline of Jupiter, so very little was birthed there either. Berry says: "Only Earth held a creative balance between the turbulence and the discipline that are necessary for creativity." On a more universal scale, the universe itself established "a creative disequilibrium expressed in the curvature of space that was sufficiently closed to establish an abiding order in the universe and sufficiently open to enable the wild creative process to continue." Therefore, the very curvature of space guarantees creativity, one more evidence of the great bias the universe holds in favor of creativity.

There is music and poetry in the universe itself—surely we hear it on planet earth. I am writing this chapter at a friend's house in San Francisco near the ocean. During a lunch break, I walked along the cliffs overlooking the bay and the Golden Gate Bridge amidst blooming flowers, singing birds, buzzing insects, singing winds, rushing waves. Who can deny the music and song, the color and shadow, the shape and richness that nature makes? Creativity begins here. We humans are latecomers to the scene. We bring a heightened imagination with powers to get things done quickly. But we should know our place and whence our amazing powers derive from.

The universe, Berry insists, is "the primary artist," and it brings into being "all our knowledge and our artistic and cultural achievements." For this reason the universe deserves to be called an "intellect-producing, aesthetic-producing, and intimacy-producing process." Were we to cut ourselves off from nature or so desecrate nature that its multiple forms of imagination and creativity were seriously diminished, we would be robbing our own imagination of its most valuable resource. As Berry puts it: "In every phase of our imaginative, aesthetic, and emotional lives we are profoundly dependent on this larger context of the surrounding world. There is no inner life without outer experience. The tragedy in the elimination of the primordial forests is not the economic but the soul-loss that is involved. For we are depriving our imagination, our emotions, and even our intellect of that overwhelming experience communicated by the wilderness." It is not just that the universe is the *origin* of our imaginations and creativity but that we depend in an ongoing way on its capacity to arouse us to give birth. The communion between the creativity of the universe and our own creativity is profound and continuous. We need to be constantly prodded and provoked by the beauty and aesthetics of the world around us.

Nature is so committed to creativity that it "abhors uniformity." The world-as-machine metaphor that dominated the modern era got us to think and act in uniform and standardized processes as machines do. But this is not the way of the natural world. Nature is biased in favor of diversity. And creativity is itself an act of diversity, as Berry reminds us: "Nature not only produces species diversity but also individual diversity. Nature produces individuals. No two days are the same, no two snowflakes, no two flowers, trees, or any other of the infinite number of life-forms."

Poet-farmer Wendell Berry writes how for his mentor, William Carlos Williams, "a poem was never merely an object of art; it was not a specialist's product. He spoke of poetry as the life force, not a 'creative act' but one of the acts of the creation, a part of the sum of

> 'All that which makes the pear ripen
> Or the poet's line
> Come true!'"

By comparing the poet's line to a pear ripening, Williams is placing *all* human creativity within its proper context: the ongoing creation of the world and, indeed, the universe.

2. Creativity Comes from Our Joys and Sorrows

If it is true that our creativity is part of the greater fabric of creative energy in the universe, an energy that has been present and active from the first millisecond of the fireball, what are some of the ways by which we come to experience and develop this creativity?

The universe brings with it great joys and great sorrows. Deep heart experiences, such as joy, delight, and ecstasy, on the one hand, and grief, sadness, and loss, on the other, trigger creativity in us. The mystics called these experiences the via positiva (the joy) and the via negativa (the suffering). These the universe gifts us with in abundance. They are integral to all our living—provided we choose to live deeply from the inside out and not to live vicariously or superficially from the outside only and to numb our experiences of life through addictions.

The thirteenth-century mystic Mechtild of Magdeburg taught that we are given two wines to drink in this life: the white wine of joy and the red wine of suffering. "Until we have drunk deeply of both," she observed, "we have not lived fully."

To understand the metaphor of the white wine of joy more deeply, think of the birth of your first child or the time you fell in love with another person. Consider how connected you felt to the universe at that moment and how connected to ancestors and the ongoing birthing process of our species. Consider the joy that ran through your heart on that special occasion. How filled your heart was on that occasion, how connected you felt to all beings, how alive, how exuberant, how awakened in all your senses. Consider times in nature: alone with the starry sky at night apart from the lights of the city; at the ocean observing its unending energy; looking into the eyes of a dog or cat or horse friend; seeing an eagle fly or a hawk soar or a gazelle run.

What can we say of these moments except that no one can take their beauty from us; no one can separate us from our deepest experiences of joy. They connect us to the depths of all things. They connect us to the universe itself from whence they come.

The same can be said of the red wine of suffering, of the pain and grief experiences that split our hearts wide open and empty us so fully that we feel nothingness is our very food. Betrayal, disappointment, death of friends and relationships and dreams, hearing the stories of evil and cruelty that overtake our species time and again—all these experiences also render us one with the universe. They trigger creativity, because they make us so vulnerable and open our heart to become its large self. Buddhist philosopher Joanna Macy says that when your heart breaks, the universe can pour through. That is how it is. When the universe pours through, so, too, does the creativity of the universe. How many comedians are funny in spite of and because of deep tragedies in their life, which have opened their souls up to the ultimate paradoxes of living? Humor and paradox are often the only ways to respond to life's sorrows with grace. Humor, too, seems built into the fabric of the universe, so filled with paradox and surprise and uncanny combinations. (Sexuality itself rates as one of these funny efforts on the part of the universe, though we often miss the humor in it by taking it too self-consciously.)

3. Creativity Comes "From and in the Heart of God"

All our spiritual traditions the world over agree that creativity flows through the human heart and that it flows from the Divine heart. Now there are many names for the Divine as we shall see. Among the Lakota people there is Wakan Tanka (The Holy One) and Tagashala (Grandfather of the rock people). There is Brahman; Allah; Tao; Goddess; Yahweh; God; Holy Spirit; Great Spirit; the One; the Creator; Buddha. In the Islamic tradition, there exists a special spiritual exercise of reciting the "ninety-nine most beautiful names for God." Among these names are many that depict Divinity in its role as the source of all creativity: The Fashioner (Al-Musawwir); The Maker (Al-Bari); The Creator (Al-Khaliq); The Expander (Al-Basit); The Constrictor (Al-Qabiz); The Maintainer (Al-Muqit); The Preserver (Al-Hafiz); The Awakener (Al-Ba'ith); The Loving (Al-Wadud); The Wise One (Al-Haki); The All-Embracing

(Al-Wase'); The Generous One (Al-Karim); The Alive (Al-Hayy); The Giver of Death (Al-Mumit); the Giver of Life (Al-Mohyi); The Restorer (Al-Muis); The Beginner (Al-Mubdi); The Source of All Goodness (Al-Barr); The Governor (Al-Waali); The First (Al-Waal); The One (Al-Wahid); The Originator (Al-Badi'); and The Light (Al-Nur).

In the medieval Christian tradition, Hildegard of Bingen asks: "Who is the Trinity?" And she replies to her question thus: "You are music. You are life." To call Divinity music is to speak to the sound that all beings are making: All atoms are busy vibrating and making music in the universe. Hildegard knew this; in fact, she heard the music. She is also addressing the first chakra, which connects us to all vibrations where universal sound is picked up. "In the beginning was the Sound." If God is music, are we tapping into God when we tune into music? If God is music, are we birthing God when we compose or play music?

Thomas Aquinas calls God "the Artist of Artists" and "the Source without a Source." He also stresses a principle behind evolution when he insists that God did not make the universe like a box and leave it but is involved in creating on a regular basis, giving existence to things. "God's work whereby God brings things into being must not be taken as the work of a craftsman who makes a box and then leaves it. For God continues to give being." Aquinas develops the idea that God is the artist par excellence when he says: "God is an artist and the universe is God's work of art." This means that every creature "can rightly be called God's work of art."

The relationship of love that the artist has for his or her work applies to God's love for creation. "All artists love what they give birth to—parents love their children; poets love their poems; craftspeople love their handiwork. How then could God hate a single thing since God is the artist of everything?"

Diversity permeates the universe because the Divine Imagination is so expansive and because the Divine Mind itself evolves. "Diversity reigns because artists have the right to change their style and make things different as time goes on." Since creatures exist both to experience the Divine goodness and to express it, diversity is necessary. "Because the Divine goodness could not be adequately represented by one creature alone, God produced many and diverse creatures, that what was wanting in one in the representation of the Divine goodness might be supplied by another." In this way "the whole universe together participates in the Divine goodness more perfectly and represents it better than any single creature whatever."

Meister Eckhart, who follows Aquinas, says that when we return "to our Source and origin all our work comes from and in the heart of God." Our hearts link up with the Divine heart, which creates the universe in a continuous fashion. This is an ancient teaching found as well in Hinduism and in Black Elk of the American Indian nations. The Bhagavad Gita says: "The Lord dwells in the hearts of all creatures, and whirls them round on the wheel of time." Thus the Divine indwelling is not a passive presence sitting inside of us; rather, it is the very Source of all movement, all activity, all creativity. Eckhart also talks of the indwelling of the Trinity as a fruitful indwelling when he writes: "God's generating is at the same time his indwelling, and his indwelling is his generating." Thus the Divine presence in us is a very fruitful presence. It produces results, it generates.

The Upanishads of India instruct us that "there is a Light that shines beyond all things on earth, beyond us all, beyond the heavens. . . . This is the Light that shines in our heart." The Light of the universe becomes our Light. The Divine is depicted as Light, and the Divine becomes our Light. In this way, the universe does indeed connect to our hearts; cosmos and psyche come together, macrocosm and microcosm. This coming together, does it not trigger our most creative experiences?

Leonard Bernstein thought so when he described his creative process in the following manner: "I sit for long nights all by myself and don't have a thought in my head. I'm dry. I'm blocked, or so it seems. I sit at the piano and just improvise—strum some chords or try a sequence of notes. And then, suddenly, I find one that hits, that suggests something else. . . . This is the most exciting moment that can happen in an artist's life. And every time it happens . . . I say 'Gratias agimus tibi.' I am grateful for that gift, for those moments, just as I can be terribly depressed by the moments in between when nothing happens. But . . . eventually those two strands will come together, a spark will fly, and I'll be off, sailing, my ego gone. I won't know my name. I won't know what time it is. Then, I'm a composer."

The Upanishads develop this theme of the coming together of the Divine and the human still further. "In the center of the castle of Brahman, our own body, there is a small shrine in the form of a lotus flower, and within can be found a small space. We should find who dwells there, and we should want to know that person." Who dwells there? "The little space within the heart is as great as this vast universe. The heavens and the earth are there, and the sun, and the moon, and the stars; fire and lightening and winds are there; and all that now is and all that is now: for the whole universe is in him and he dwells within our heart." Notice that our hearts are so vast that the entire universe occupies only a "little space"! How amazing an image. What a vast reservoir of being our hearts and creative minds represent.

Moreover, the Divine One dwells within us while the whole universe dwells within him or her. Such vastness we encounter when we open up to what is. This is the same understanding that Jesus had when he said, "The kingdom/queendom of God is within you." All of creation is in us, *and* the Divine Godhead who dwells in creation is in us. Eckhart echoes this sense of the vastness of our heart's knowledge when he says: "The inward work always includes in itself all size, all breadth and all length."

Black Elk also addresses the presence of the Divine within us and its relation to the universe and its powers when he says: "The heart is a sanctuary at the center of which there is a little space, wherein the Great Spirit dwells, and this is the Eye. This is the Eye of the Great Spirit by which he sees all things, and through which we see him." When we return to this center, true peace manifests itself in our soul. "The first peace, which is the most important, is that which comes within the souls of men when they realize their relationship, the oneness, with the universe and all its powers, and when they realize that at the center of the universe dwells Wakan Tanka, and that this center is really everywhere, it is within each of us. This is the real peace and the others are but reflections of this." By tapping into this "real peace," into our oneness with the universe, we become peace and carry on peace. We become creative and carry on creativity.

An ancient Mesoamerican poem speaks to the work of the artist in a manner that flows beautifully from the words of Black Elk.

The true artist draws out all from his or her heart.
The good painter is wise,
God is in his heart.
He puts divinity into things;
he converses with his own heart.

Thus the work of the artist in all of us is to be in dialogue with our hearts, for God dwells therein. And the work of the artist is nothing less than to "put divinity into things." That is to say, we are indeed co-creating when we create— we are not only co-creating *with* God and the powers of creation, we are actually co-creating God and the powers of creation! They happen through us—just as they happen through other species in the universe and through other expressions of time and space. Eckhart says: "There where God speaks the creatures, there God is." And "God becomes as creatures express God." How noble our creativity becomes! How sacred and holy. How full of responsibility.

But there is still more deep wisdom being taught here, namely the *how* of our bringing the Divine forward in our creativity. This happens to the extent that we "converse with our own heart." To be in touch with our hearts *is* to be in touch with the heart of the universe and the heart of the Divine Creator. Is this why the indigenous peoples around the world put so much faith in the drum as the basic instrument of prayer? Because the drumbeat bespeaks the beat of the heart—not just our human heart but the heart of the universe, the heart of the Creator. To return to this heart is the purpose of all prayer and all meditation. When we return to this heart, the Divine creativity flows again.

The indigenous people of African understood this. Dancing to the beat of the drum releases both breath and spirit. It connects us to cosmic forces, which in turn energize us and bless us. African scholar Dona Marimba Richards speaks as follows: "As in ritual, in music the human and the Divine meet. . . . Through dance we experience reality as immediate to us; that is, we are identified with the universe. . . . We have experienced cosmic relationship. . . . Dance, for us, is a religious expression. When we dance, through rhythm, we express ourselves as cosmic beings. Music transcends us to ultimate realities." Art is not something done *for* another or *to* another. Art is everybody participating, that is, when ritual is real, when the whole community participates. No one can pray vicariously. No one can sing or chant or dance in our place. We are all meant to participate because each of us must find the "center," the "eye of God," wherein the true peace flows. We are all meant to tap into the creative energy of the Holy One, the Artist of Artists and the Source without a Source.

Among the indigenous people of the world there is still great confidence that our species can indeed tap into that Source, that the human world and the great universe can come together because *they have come together.* Our ancestors celebrated these practices and brought about marvelous things. We can do the same and with the help of the ancestors.

All artists have to relearn these truths. All artists have to let go of the modern world's silly and reductionist notions that art is for art's sake or art is for fame's sake or art is for venting's sake and start serving the heart of God once again. Artists need an inner life just like everyone else. They also need an outer life, that is to say, a cosmology, an awareness of how we got here and what "here" constitutes in its holy vastness and its unimaginable diversity and creativity. A return to our origins is long overdue for all professionals but especially for artists, because their task is to lead the rest of us in moving through perilous times of cynicism, boredom, and despair.

Since, as the Mesoamerican poet declares, it is the work of the artist to draw "all out from his or her heart," all the more reason for artists to *grow their hearts*. To do whatever it takes to make one's heart larger, to deepen their knowledge of compassion and therefore of praise for what is beautiful and of criticism of what is ugly and unjust. To grow in compassion is to grow in our hearts and to allow more of the Divine in and more of the Divine through the heart. It is also to return our gifts of insight and beauty and criticism back to the community, a return of beauty for beauty, blessing for blessing, gift for gift.

{four}

what happens when the creative spirit and we co-create?

 Many people have offered insights as to the primal power of creativity, its meaning, and its ways of coming to expression in and through us. The mystics, in particular, who are poets of the soul and its interaction with the Divine, relate the relationship of the depths of our soul-work and our creative work to the depths of the Divine work working in the world.

As we approach Spirit and Spirit approaches us, we must become more like Spirit. If we are to be co-creators, then Spirit and ourselves must share much in common. Meister Eckhart teaches this when he insists that "love can only be where there is equality." A certain kind of equality must exist between Spirit and us. This helps to explain the depths of suffering and brokenness that we often go through as human beings and as creative people. Such brokenness opens us up to Spirit and makes us freer like Spirit is, freer to welcome Spirit and to recognize Spirit when it shows up and chooses to reveal itself to us or through us. We become instruments of Spirit, or, as Eckhart puts it, "God becomes the place where God wants to act."

Hildegard of Bingen puts it this way: "The marvels of God are not brought forth from one's self. Rather, it is more like a chord, a sound that is played. The tone does not come out of the chord itself, but rather through the touch of the musician." God plays us like a musical instrument. "I am, of course, the lyre and harp of God's kindness." Because "Divinity is aimed at humanity," we are "exalted with the vocation of creation," and we can receive the Divine powers and graces and give birth accordingly.

Indeed, in Hildegard's vision, our giving birth is no less than nature's giving birth in trees, rocks, and orchards. "This is how the person becomes a flowering orchard. The person who does good works is indeed this orchard bearing good fruit. And this is just like the earth with its ornamentation of stone and blossoming trees." We are recipients of God's and nature's talents for creation, since "God gave to humankind the talent to create with all the world." We do not create in a vacuum but "with all the world," that is, within the context of creation and the cosmos. And we create *with* the world—not in an antagonistic relationship *against* the world or in opposition to it or in neglect of it.

Let us turn to the teaching of the mystics in this chapter. What exactly happens when the Divine and the human come together in our creative activity?

1. "The Fierce Power of Imagination Is a Gift from God"

In the Kabbalah, the medieval Jewish mystical work, we are instructed that "the fierce power of imagination is a gift from God." To call imagination a "fierce power" is to warn us that we are wrestling with wild forces when we enter the arena of creativity. A wrestling match not unlike Jacob struggling with an angel can be anticipated. Or David and Goliath. Did not David outwit Goliath? Was his victory not a victory of human imagination and spirit over mere brute strength? Is that not why the story is told and retold through generations with such power—because the "meek will inherit the earth" and because, according to Mary the mother of Jesus, "God has pulled down princes from their thrones and exalted the lowly, sending the rich away empty while filling the hungry with good things"? (Luke 1:52–53).

Just how fierce is this power of imagination? Consider that a few years ago in a county in New Hampshire the fundamentalists were elected the majority in the school board. Their first decree was to declare that henceforth no teacher in a public school in that district was allowed to use the word "imagination" in the classroom. Fear. Fear of imagination. Fear of its fierceness. When I inquired of some citizens of the area what it was that the fundamentalists were afraid of, they responded: "Satan. Satan lives in the imagination." Well, that is certainly true. Satan lives there. God also lives there (if we let Her), and everything possible and impossible. Being and nonbeing dwell in our imaginations. Thomas Aquinas says the human mind is "infinite." That's the wonder and the power of imagination—it contains all things. It is huge. It is bigger than the cosmos. But we need courage to combat the fear that faces the fierceness of imagination and wants to shrink from the wild reality of it all.

Notice that the Kabbalah counsels us that imagination is a "gift from God." That is saying a lot. It is telling us not to fear. Our powers come from Divinity itself. Grow up. Take responsibility. Get strong. Become adult about it all. Develop adult prayer and cease wallowing in childish (as distinct from childlike) projections that produce anxiety and fear. Yes, wrestle with the demons—don't give them so much power that they put an end to the best of human and Divine powers. Understanding that our capacity for image-making is a gift from God derives from the teaching that we humans are made in the "image and likeness of God" ("imago dei"). It raises the question of our intimate relationship to the Divine.

Fundamentalists who engage in imagination-bashing might take note of the following fact: The etymological origin for the word "hell" (the real place where Satan dwells?) is *helan,* an old English word that means "to conceal" (in

Latin, *celare*). In other words, hell is our place of concealment. Hell, then, is our refusal to create and our deadening
the imagination of others. But if hell is concealment, then
heaven must be creativity itself. Heaven would be the place
of revelation, of unveiling, of telling the truth. Eckhart
said: "The purpose of a word is to reveal." That is the purpose of all imagination.

Teacher and painter, poet and potter M. C. Richards
asks: "Isn't this what we try to do in our artistic work with
the clay: to bring something to light, to manifest, to reveal?
A form, an intention, a question, a relationship, a search, a
hope, a defeat, a concealment . . . ?" Why would we want to
cover up revelation? (Unless, of course, we felt that *all* revelation has already happened—which is a downer, to say
the least. As if every new child and every new relationship
and every new learning experience in our lives is not a new
revelation.)

But it is not just religious fundamentalists who are scared
of the fierce and wild power of imagination. Academic fundamentalists are also. I know a professor who received his
doctoral degree just a few years ago from a very prestigious
university on the West Coast. He did his doctorate in
English literature on "The Sacred in D. H. Lawrence." He
received two warnings from his doctoral committee: I)
You must not use the word "soul" in your dissertation, but,
if you must, you have to put quotation marks around it.
(I asked if D. H. Lawrence put quotation marks around the

word "soul" in his work.) 2) You are forbidden to use the word "imagination" in the dissertation since it is a "romantic" concept.

It is amazing the biases that some academics bring to so-called education. Do we really expect education to reinvent itself when it holds more in common with fundamentalism than with the history of ideas and learning in our culture? Is academia stuck in a cycle of creating its own kind of "hell," or place of concealment, by resisting soul and imagination? Is academia committed to the suppression of revelation? M. C. Richards holds to a more ancient understanding of education when she writes: "To teach is to show. A showing is a revelation of more than we can see with our physical eyes; it shines into our understanding, *schon*. The beautiful is that which is revealed. And what is revealed?

> *Gold lustre swimmers and copper red fish*
> *angel nibbling at the shore*
> *and our clay feet walking on water."*

The only good news I take from this sorry tale of academic fundamentalism is an affirmation of an insight I have been acting on for five years: We need new models of education, forms of education in which the words "soul" and "imagination" are not banished but are honored and deepened and acted upon. This story very much confirmed whatever blood, sweat, tears, and sacrifice have gone into our University of Creation Spirituality these past five years, located as we are in the shadow of the august educational institution that is so unnerved by soul-talk and imagination-talk.

Our government has often declared its belief in the fierceness of imagination in actions it has taken to stifle imagination of indigenous peoples of our land. Consider how our anxious government forbade the sundance ceremony and other rituals of the indigenous peoples for over one hundred years—it was only during the Carter presidency that laws that forbade certain rituals were formally repealed. This fear of ritual is, ironically, an affirmation of the power of ritual, a power that even our government recognizes, albeit perversely, by forbidding it.

Another example of our country's awareness of the fierce power of imagination was its efforts to take the drum away from the African slaves who were brought to this land. By taking the drum away, slave masters felt they could more effectively control the slaves. They recognized the power in the drumming, dancing, chanting, and connecting to the cosmic forces that occurs in rituals wherein the drum was allowed to lead and to speak its power. While the drum was denied the slaves, imagination overcame this loss, and the drum reappeared as the cadence in the spoken word of the preacher in the black church and in alternative forms of musical expression, such as the invention of jazz and blues in black culture. Imagination would not be denied. It found an outlet for its truth.

2. Is "Imagination" Another Word for "Soul"?

Among the Celts, "imagination" means soul. Celtic scholar John O'Donohue points out that in the Celtic way of seeing the world, the "soul" "is the place where the imagination lives." The imagination operates at a threshold where light and dark, visible and invisible, possibility and fact come together. "The linear, controlling, external mind will never even glimpse" the gift that imagination is. The revelations of nature come to us by way of imagination—that is, what expands the soul. In a culture where anthropocentrism does not reign, imagination still does. For imagination needs the cosmos to feed on. It longs for relationships that stretch the soul.

What is imagination? French philosopher Gaston Bachelard has much to say about our imaginations. "Man lives by images," he writes, for "only images can set verbs in motion again." In other words, images wake us up from our slumber and our deadness. We are put into motion *again*. The imagination seldom sleeps; it is very busy seeking the new: "The imagination is ceaselessly imagining and enriching itself with new images." The imagination is bigger than reality, for "there will always be more things in a closed, than in an open, box. To verify images kills them, and it is always more enriching to *imagine* than to *experience*." (My mother used to tell us as children that more than half the fun of anything was looking forward to it.) Images challenge us, indeed "images are more challenging than ideas," Bachelard believes.

Imagination feeds hope, for there is "a sort of innate optimism in all works of the imagination." And the goal of imagination is nothing less than liberation itself, liberation being "a special characteristic of the activity of the imagination," which liberates us from the forces that hold us imprisoned in the "here." Imagination is so vast, so large, so free that it grows our souls and allows us to "contemplate grandeur." The cosmos our imagination births is even larger than the physical cosmos. We become transported "outside the immediate world to a world that bears the mark of infinity. . . . Isn't imagination alone able to enlarge indefinitely the images of immensity? It takes us to the space of elsewhere."

I love that phrase—"the space of elsewhere." Imagination takes us to nothingness, to emptiness, to *what is not yet* and therefore to *what might still be*. The space of elsewhere, indeed. No wonder the prophets relied so heavily on imagination.

My soul and my imagination were awakened this morning when I walked above the churning waters of San Francisco Bay. The waters were churning, churning, churning as they crashed against the rocks and the shore and one another. All this energy, all this creativity. *Every wave is an act of creativity* on the part of nature. Where is all this churning, where is all this creativity coming from? It comes from the universe—i.e., that place where the dynamics for energy comes from. From the moon that sets the tides that set in motion the waters. From the sun that unleashes the winds that move the waves that churn the waters. From the waters and the forces that made waters to happen. From the land, rugged and mountain-filled and valley-filled below the waters. From the power of gravity that binds and loosens the rhythms of contraction and expansion. This is the nature of creativity—ours and the rest of nature's. Creativity *is* a cosmic habit into which our species has been invited to participate and even to explore in modes of understanding. And to praise in all new modes of appreciation and gratitude.

If we do not have a living imagination and are not busy feeding and nourishing imagination, then we simply lack soul. I feel sorry for fundamentalists of any kind who exclude powers of creativity and then wonder why fear and control addictions take over their life. All fascism wants to kill imagination and make control into God. That way lies cynicism as well. We have to learn to trust the universe and its creative powers. And to love them. The modern era's attempt to "master" (Descartes's word and Francis Bacon's) nature is a pitiful, arrogant, demeaning, dead-end joke. Trust, not master. Dance with the rhythms of creativity, don't sit on the sidelines seeking to control it. Whether that compulsion to control comes from religious fundamentalism or academic fundamentalism, it leads to the same ennui for living and the same fixation on control. It also opens the door to cynicism and the desire to escape life by way of addictions, be they drugs, alcohol, shopping, TV, or more.

Creativity—and with it creation—is still very much in

process. There is a river of creativity running through all things, all relationships, all beings, all corners and centers of this universe. We are here to join it, to get wet, to jump in, to ride these rapids, wild and sacred as they be.

3. Creativity as the Holy Spirit at Work

Meister Eckhart equates that river with the Holy Spirit itself. Psalm Forty-six reads as follows: "There is a river whose streams refresh the city of God, and it sanctifies the dwelling of the Most High." Eckhart comments on this Psalm by citing John's Gospel (John 7:38) which promises that "living waters will flow" to those whose faith is, as Eckhart says, "enlightened by divine love and who prove it by their good works." Creativity *is* our "good work," and it is meant to emanate from our "Divine love." The Spirit works by "quick and wonderful deeds" and can be called an "intoxication" because of its "quick emanation." The Spirit "springs" and "rises" and "presses" and "leaps" inside of us even as it intoxicates us.

Why is this? Because there is such a profound interconnection between our emptying and the Spirit's filling. "The Spirit flows just as completely into the soul as the soul empties itself in humility and expands itself to receive him." The Spirit flows and flows, fills and fills, and "cannot keep from flowing into every place where it finds space and flows just as extensively as the space it finds there."

What is required to respond to this flowing river of the

Spirit of Creativity in addition to emptying ourselves to be ready? A focusing is required—and a uniting of all our powers. "On the outside the soul is preserved from encumbrances and on the inside it is united in all its powers." Aquinas calls this uniting of our powers "contemplation," and he says wisdom is the one who brings it about. Maybe this is why wisdom and creativity go together so intimately, as Hildegard has said: "There is wisdom in all creative works." It also explains why meditation of some kind is essential for the creative process to flow and to flow from its deepest source. Eckhart repeats this warning: "The soul must be brought together and solidified to the noble powers found within it if the soul is to receive the divine 'river' that fills it and causes it to rejoice."

Eckhart compares this happening to the coming of the Holy Spirit at the time of Pentecost, for "the Apostles were gathered together and enclosed when they received the Holy Spirit." This coming of the Spirit in our acts of creativity is compared to the coming of the Holy Spirit over Mary to conceive the Christ Child. "The work that is 'with,' 'outside,' and 'above' the artist must become the work that is 'in' him, taking form within him, in other words, to the end that he may produce a work of art, in accordance with the verse 'the Holy Spirit shall come upon thee' (Luke 1:35), that is, so that the 'above' may become 'in.'" Eckhart recognizes that "the Son comes into being in us" when the Spirit works in us. Thus we are birthing Divinity—nothing less than the

Cosmic Christ (or Buddha nature)—when we create. Just as Mary did.

Aquinas also spoke of our creativity as the coming of the Holy Spirit: "The same Spirit who hovered over the waters at the beginning of creation hovers over the mind of the artist at work." The power of creation itself becomes our power at such moments.

Solitude is a necessary part of the filling with grace that the Holy Spirit brings to us. Eckhart says: "God leads his bride, that is, the soul, away from the dignity and nobility of all creatures to a solitary desert and into himself, and he himself speaks into the soul's heart. This means that he makes the soul equal in grace to himself. For this noble deed the soul has to gather and close itself up." It follows that when we birth what is within us we are co-workers with God, for "if I speak God's word, then I am a co-worker with God, and grace is mixed up with a creature, that is, with myself." Grace and ourselves get mixed up together in acts of creativity and co-creation.

4. Creativity Brings Joy with It

Notice how Eckhart declares that creativity "causes the soul to rejoice"—it brings rejoicing and joy with it. That is certainly my experience. I am happiest when I am caught up and lost in acts of creativity. When I lose all sense of time and even place and self-consciousness, being lost in the temple, the Divine space of perpetual creativity—that brings great joy. A joy no one can take from us.

The Upanishads of ancient India recognize the Divine joy that comes with creativity when they declare: "Know the nature of creating. Where there is joy, there is creating. Know the nature of joy. Where there is the Infinite, there is joy." Thus the joy of creating comes from the Godself. "The rapid or quick-flowing river has caused the city of God to rejoice" (Psalm 46:4, Eckhart's translation). And the city, says Eckhart, is the soul. But it is also the greater community. Thus Eckhart invokes the psalmist on this point who declares that "the rapid or quick-flowing river has caused the city of God to rejoice" (Psalm 46:4). Perhaps Eckhart has in mind the joy that derives from the gathering of the forces of nature that happens in a city when artists gather.

As co-creators, we ought to be attuned to the basic energy of nature itself. That energy includes joy. Recently I received a letter from a Colorado woman who attended a workshop I conducted there. In the letter, she tells me that she took a "sabbatical" from peace activism to go on a prolonged retreat. She writes: "I had discovered that I needed time away to do the work of inner disarmament. And, if I were to survive periods of incarceration, I needed to create a strong inner 'poustinia.' So I moved into a small, one room cabin in the forest. I only had to work one day a week, in town, to support myself. I spent my days walking in the forest, sitting by streams, watching and listening. Mostly listening. After about two years, nature and silence taught me this: that at the core of all that exists, e.g., at the core of every blade of grass, hanging icicle, quarreling marmot, beaver, soaring eagle, quacking duck, squirrel, fox, howling coyote, quivering aspen leaf, and melting snow flake, there exists an energy/vibration of joy. Not unlike a giggle. And if we wish to take our cues from creation and work in harmony with her, then we, too, have to be in that energy of joy. YES!"

Native-American and Franciscan teacher Jose Hobday talks of the relationship between joy and simple living: "Simple living calls us to reverence for all that is. We walk with gratitude and wonder. We do not allow ourselves to become dulled and insensitive to the beauty of the world. We learn to worship." One's capacity for "inner extravagance" and for "adventure" increases when one can learn the discipline of simple living. Hobday promises: "You'll be amazed at how much fun you have and how much freedom simplicity gives you. You'll experience a kind of joy of heart."

5. We Must Give Birth

There is a kind of imperative to give birth, to create. Perhaps it derives from our being made in the image and likeness of the Creator God. Eckhart names this obligation in a most telling manner: "What is my name? What is your name? What is God's name? Our name is: that we must be born. And the Creator's name is: to bear." To create is to share. To share is to give back gift for gift, blessing for blessing. "Human beings should be communicative and emanative with all the gifts they have received from God. . . . If human beings have something that they do not bestow on others, they are not good. People who do not bestow on others spiritual things and whatever bliss is in them have never been spiritual. People are not to receive and keep them for themselves alone, but they should share themselves and pour forth everything they possess in their bodies and souls as far as possible and whatever others desire of them." Notice that Eckhart is warning us of the sacrifice—both bodily and personally—that is required of the giving away of our creativity. A "pouring forth" of our bodies and our souls may be required of us, one more instance wherein we are reminded of the *courage* and strong heart it takes to follow the path of creativity.

Aquinas also emphasizes the imperative dimension to our creativity. He compares our situation to the earth itself that was given the command in Genesis to "bring forth" (Genesis 1:11). "Now the earth is fertile.... And so the hearers of this teaching ... must be fertile, so that the words of wisdom that they receive will be fruitful in them, as Jesus said (Luke 8:15): 'The seed that fell on good ground ...'" To be connected with the Christ as Source is to glorify the Creator. "We are in Christ when we bear fruit from him, and the Creator is glorified from our bearing fruit." This is how eager Divinity is that we create: The Divine glory depends on it.

6. Creativity Takes Trust and Courage

Creativity takes courage—courage to explore one's deepest self and to let in the depths of the world's struggles and joys, torments and agony. Rilke put it this way: "Works of art always spring from those who have faced the danger, gone to the very end of an experience, to the point beyond which no human being can go. The further one dares to go, the more decent, the more personal, the more unique a life becomes. . . . This sort of derangement, which is peculiar to us, must go into our work." The artist, he dares tell us, faces derangement itself. Artists need encouragement, the building up of courage, that community can lend us. The artist in each of us needs and deserves attention in order to build up the heart.

Eckhart explains why so few people take the path of creativity when he says that it is lack of trust that keeps us wallowing in our noncreative state: "Why is it that some people do not bear fruit? It is because they are busy clinging to their egotistical attachments and so afraid of letting go and letting be that they have no trust either in God or in themselves."

Gaston Bachelard believes that trust derives from our cosmology or lack thereof. Our trust or lack of trust betrays our relationship to the universe. We learn trust from observing the confidence that other beings hold in the universe. Trust can begin with the simple act of examining a bird's nest, for "when we examine a nest, we place ourselves at the origin of confidence in the world, we receive a beginning of confidence, an urge toward cosmic confidence. Would a bird build its nest if it did not have its instinct for confidence in the world?" A nest is a sign of optimism. It "knows nothing of the hostility of the world. . . . The experience of the hostility of the world—and consequently, our dreams of defense and aggressiveness—come much later." Trust begins at a very early age, with our own experiences of nesting. "In its germinal form, therefore, all of life is well-being. Being starts with well-being. . . . A dreamer might say that the world is the nest of mankind. For the world is a nest and an immense power holds the inhabitants of the world in this nest." And with this trust, creativity and imagination come to life. For "mankind's nest, like his world, is never finished. And imagination helps us to continue it." Our nest is a work in progress. And progress requires trust.

Fear and distrust prevent us from creating—fear and a puny heart (from which we get the word "pusillanimity"). Aquinas sees pusillanimity as resulting in a grave sin of omission. "Pusillanimity makes people fall short of what is proportionate to their power." This is why the servant who buried his money and refused to trade it did so "through fainthearted fear" and was punished by his master (Matthew 25:14–30). We are to use the gifts we have been given. "If one fails to use the ability that one derives either from a good natural disposition, or from science or from external fortune, for virtue, then one becomes guilty of pusillanimity." There is a *coldness* in the person who refuses to create, a refusal to share one's gifts.

Does humility dictate that we hide our creative gifts? "If

anyone despises the good that they have received from God, this—far from being a proof of humility—shows them to be ungrateful. And from this contempt acedia results." It is telling that Aquinas traces acedia, or cynicism, boredom and ennui, to the refusal of the artist to do his or her art. This is another way of saying that the artist is here to wake us all up. If the artist fails to do his or her art, then acedia results. We all fall asleep. Couchpotatoitis takes over a culture. One reason creativity takes courage is that the Holy Spirit is no small force to let into our lives. This is, after all, the very Spirit that "drives the heavens." It is powerful, it is far bigger than us, it drives the forces of nature from fireball to galaxies, from supernovas to ocean waves, from the movement of the earth to the whirling of the stars.

Furthermore, we so long for this Spirit to fill our souls that when we encounter it we often dance with madness. "The divine countenance is capable of maddening and driving all souls out of their senses with longing for it," Eckhart observes. Wildness is everywhere in our relationship with the Spirit. Who is in charge here? Certainly not we. Yet there is method behind the madness, peace within the wildness, love within the yearning that is mutual between Spirit and us. For, Eckhart promises, "when the Spirit does this by its very divine nature it is thereby drawing all things to itself." How good it is to be drawn along with all things into the intimacy of the Godself! How natural a place to be. We find repose there. In the Spirit. With the Spirit. Sharing the Spirit's work.

It is little wonder that the psychologist Rollo May wrote a book called *The Courage to Create*, which built on theologian Paul Tillich's book *The Courage to Be*. Being and creating go together. Both take a large heart. Creativity stands up to temptations to guilt for disturbing the peace. Many in a culture do not want to hear about innovation and new directions that creativity unleashes. Creativity takes courage.

7. To Create Is to Behold, Waken, and Awaken

Hildegard teaches that when we give birth the Holy Spirit works through us to "resurrect and awaken everything that is." This is, indeed, the Spirit's work—to awaken all things. That is the artist's work also: to resurrect and awaken all that is and all we perceive. The artist does this first by waking up oneself to what is. Then he or she can awaken others. The artist finds himself or herself vulnerable to beings and events and takes the time to experience them in depth. In this way, we wake up to being, we awaken to what is and its great depth and mystery. Being is holy. "Isness is God," says Eckhart. This truth of the deep-down holiness of things ought to be enough to awaken all of us from our slumber.

The artist teaches us to *behold*—to hold being, to hold being in respect, even in reverence, to hold being as something sacred, as something alive and imbued with Spirit's intentions and love. To hold being up—all of it, the joy and the sorrow, the beauty and the ugly—so that others might behold it first. And act next. These actions might take the expression of *praise* when we behold the wonder and glory of being; or of *interfering* when we behold the destruction of being; or of *healing* when we behold the victims of the struggles that being is heir to.

All this holding, beholding, and holding up of being takes courage—an inner strength to put being first, to resist the fads and external allurements of a culture that is far from putting being first but prefers to accord the place of honor to superficialities and trivia. It takes a big heart and courage to see the big picture and learn about it and study it and grow into the largeness of being. I recently saw a slogan that I like a lot: "Quit whining and read." "Study," which I define as the disciplined pursuit of our holy curiosity, is a necessary part of remaining alive and remaining creative and resisting cynicism. We must pursue truth, work at it, sweat for it, just as we have to work at keeping our bodies healthy. The mind requires no less attention. The imagination can grow stale and flabby and weak if we do not seek out healthy food with which to nourish it.

People ask me: "Why do you write so much? Are you addicted to seeing your name in print?" Hardly. I write because I am driven to know, and writing for me is a wonderful way to learn. I also write because the discipline it takes is good for my mind; it keeps it in shape and youthful and alive. I believe in exercising the virtue of curiosity. I write because of the joy involved in giving birth. Writing and the reading and study that accompany it are joyful experiences for me.

The Spirit comes to me when I write and learn. I think it always has.

Anaïs Nin once said: "We write to taste life twice." I agree. I think we write to taste life twice, and we paint and dance and sing and compose and do all art "to taste life twice." This opportunity to taste life twice is an invitation to go deeper, to miss nothing, to tell others, to experience the joy a second time in the telling and in handing on the depth and the mystery of life. When we behold, we become so struck by what is that we want to share. We call that sharing "art."

8. Co-Creation: The Dignity of Divine Causality Working Through Us

Who is God? What is Divinity about? God is above all a generative being. Eckhart calls God "pure generation" and the "life of all things." We who are made in God's likeness are also generators and life-givers. Creating is our imitating of Divinity. We are here to imitate Divinity. Nothing less. All of creation is generative. Why would the human species, so powerfully endowed with imagination, not also be generative? But we do not generate alone, we generate in communion with the Divine who dwells *and* generates within us. We tap into the work of the Creator whose power is "unceasingly glowing and burning with all the Divine wealth, all the Divine sweetness, all the Divine bliss."

Eckhart honors the receptivity that occurs when we receive God, but he insists that "it is better for God to become fruitful within the person." Why is this? "Because becoming fruitful as a result of the gift is the only gratitude for the gift. The Spirit is a wife through the continuously bearing gratitude in which it bears Jesus back into God's fatherly heart." When we respond creatively to our gifts, "we bear much fruit, and the fruit is of good size. It is no less nor more than God himself." We bear this fruit daily "a hundred times or a thousand times or countless times, giving birth and becoming fruitful out of the most noble foundation of all." This puts God into rapture and unimaginable joy. Furthermore, this is the fruit "that remains," as the Christ in John's Gospel promised. What is the fruit that remains? That which is inborn from deep within us. This fruit, these gifts that remain, are our Thank You. They are also our challenge to death itself. They remain beyond death. They are not lost in the universe. They join the other gifts, the other beings, of the universe. Beauty is added to beauty; grace to grace; blessing to blessing; thank you to thank you. Creation continues. Evolution, we would say today, goes on.

Thomas Aquinas teaches that the universe is not governed by God alone but that God shares the governance with other creatures. "Secondary causes are the executors of Divine providence. The world is governed through secondary causes." We, then, are sharers in the governing of the universe. All our human experience indicates that a balanced and working project that is also beautiful to behold requires an architect, so why wouldn't our universe require one? Aquinas sees God as the supreme architect of the universe.

Creatures enter into the work of the architecture of the universe in a big way. "From an abundance of Divine goodness have creatures been endowed with the dignity of causality." It is precisely as causes that every creature "attains the Divine likeness." In our creativity we are "communicating to another being the perfection that we possess," and in this action we actually imitate the Divine action. "Every creature strives, by its activity, to communicate its own perfect being, in its own fashion, to another; and in this it tends toward an imitation of the Divine causality." Built within every creature is this yearning, this drive, to communicate itself to others. Creativity will not be denied. It lurks deep within.

That we imitate the Divine causality is no small thing; that we share it with all other creatures is no small thing. We are not alone in the universe after all. We are not without meaning and without purpose, a chance happening. We have a purpose. It is to imitate the Divine causality. To bring things into being and to awaken beings and praise their accomplishments. Indeed, this force of creativity constitutes our being the image and likeness of the Creator. "Although a created being tends to the Divine likeness in many ways, this one, whereby it seeks the Divine likeness by being the cause of others, takes the ultimate place. Hence Dionysius says, that 'of all things it is more Divine to become a co-worker with God' in accord with the statement of the Apostle: 'We are God's co-workers'" (I Corinthians 3:9).

Our creativity is so grounded in Divinity because Divinity is the source of all generativity. Aquinas continues: "In God is the generative power. . . . The generative power is really identical with the Divine nature, so that the nature is essentially included in it." Indeed, "there is in God perfect fecundity." So close is Divinity to creativity that God's wisdom drives God to create. "God's wisdom is that of artists, whose knowledge of what they make is practical as well as theoretical: 'Thou has made all things in wisdom' (Psalm 104:24)." In fact, "Art, the idea of a thing to be made in the mind of the maker, is possessed most authentically by God." Just as all artists take satisfaction in their work, so, too, God took satisfaction in the works of creation, and this is why the Scriptures say "God saw that it was good." All of creation is "God's work of art." Thus we are all born of the mind and intention, indeed the love, of the Divine artist at work. Aquinas observes that artists do their work out of love—their spirit moves over their materials with love— and they take great joy in the work that they give birth to.

Our minds are truly infinite in their capacities. Our imaginations know no limits. "The intellect is the form of forms, because it has a form that is not determined to one thing alone, as is the case with a stone, but has a capacity for all forms." We give birth to form and to non-form, to familiar forms and to genuinely new forms. We are capable of an unlimited number of forms! We are not restricted to any one form. "My heart has become capable of every form," writes the Sufi mystic Ibn Al-Arabi.

There is a profound sense of freedom, therefore, in our acts of creativity. They take us back to what Eckhart calls our "unborn self"—as free as we were before we were born, free in mind, free in will, free to become what we will become. This sense of freedom is part of the "rush" that often accompanies creative activity.

9. "Art Is the Conversation Between Lovers"

The medieval Sufi mystic Hafiz declares that "art is the conversation between lovers." This insight would seem to echo the emphasis we have seen previously on the heart and art. If art is central to our hearts, then art meets art where heart meets heart. The musician reaches out to touch the hearts of her listeners. The painter reaches out to touch the hearts of his observers. The playwright and actor reach out to grab the hearts of their audience. And so it goes.

But the hearts of the lovers that art touches are not just the human lovers in our lives. God, too, is a lover. God's art has touched our hearts, and our art touches the Divine heart. How are we lovers with God? How much play goes on between us? How many fairly fought fights? How much laughter and teasing and joint dreaming and scheming? Just how does our art constitute a conversation with God as lover? The effort we put into our work is our gift to God.

Otto Rank taught that ultimately every gift the artist gives is a gift to God. We cannot get away from it. Our many gifts are God-given and so their return is a God-return. No one who gives a gift wants to see it unused. Nor does God. So all our gifts are a return on God's gift-giving, an act of generous gratitude for the gifts of our intelligence, our observation, our imagination, our very being in the world and the universe itself.

Lovers want to gift one another with gifts, to surprise one another and to make one another happy. Hafiz is wise to apply these actions of mutuality and gratitude and play to our relationship with the Divine. Art becomes the language, the conversation at play between the God-who-is-lover and the human-who-is-lover. It raises the human from being merely the "beloved" to also being a lover. And it raises God from being just a "lover" to also being the "beloved." To be a co-creator is to be a lover. In this way our work becomes an act of love, a work of art, a conversation between lovers. That is a good thing, for it sacralizes our work and renders its results grace-like.

10. The Next Revolution Will Be a Revolution in Aesthetics

In the Preface I invoked an essay on "Postmodern Blackness" by African-American philosopher bell hooks. hooks lays out the stakes for the awakening that art itself needs to undergo today and declares that the revolution of the future will be a revolution in aesthetics. Aesthetics is the bridge, she believes, between the "black underclass" and the dominant classes.

It is striking to hear a call for an aesthetic revolution when the modern era was so devoid of aesthetics! Descartes, the principal philosopher of that era, developed an entire philosophy with no philosophy of aesthetics. As a culture we put aesthetics, which is an interest in the beautiful, on the back burner. Efficiency ruled in the industrial age, not aesthetics. Aesthetics was pretty much relegated to the very wealthy, who had leisure time and excess money on their hands. It came as a payoff at the end of one's climb up the ladder of success. Aesthetics was reduced to investments that filled the void in the soul.

What is being said by bell hooks is very revolutionary. She is saying that we humans cannot live without beauty and that it is beauty that binds us together, that cuts through all the classes. She is by no means alone in her call for an awakening to beauty. It is an ancient, premodern understanding that the Divine and beauty go together, indeed that "beauty" is another name for the Divine, and that all beauty calls us back to the primordial, Divine beauty. In Egypt, around 1550 B.C.E., hymns were created to the god Aten. They go like this:

> *Beautiful you rise, O eternal living god!*
> *You are radiant, lovely, powerful. . . .*
> *You nourish the hearts by your beauty. . . .*

> *Beautiful you rise in heaven's horizon,*
> *O eternal, living Creator!*
> *You fill every land with your beauty. . . .*
> *All eyes are on your beauty until you set.*

An ancient Mesoamerican poem praises the beauty of nature along with the beauty of the human poet.

> The beautiful flowers, the beautiful songs
> come from the interior of heaven. . . .
> Your beautiful son
> is a golden rattlesnake-bird,
> you send it aloft most beautifully. . . .
> Have you by chance spoken with the God?

Clearly, the poet is saying that all who tap into beauty and put it into the world are in conversation with God, the author of beauty in nature.

In Sufism, the Zikr is a remembrance ritual whose purpose is above all *to remember beauty*, the daily beauty that we can so easily take for granted. "The mind often becomes plagued and can deny the all-pervading beauty of God" if the Zikr is forgotten. The prophet Muhammad declared: "God is beautiful, and He loves beauty; all that is beautiful comes from the beauty of God." The Christian mystic Thomas Aquinas very much concurs when he says: "The highest beauty is in the Godhead. . . . God is beauty itself, beautifying all things. The Creator of beauty has set up all the beauty of things." He calls God "supersubstantial beauty," who "bestows beauty on all created beings." God's beauty does not waver: "God is a fountain of total beauty." All beings are participating in the Divine beauty, and they possess a kind of " 'sheen,' a reflection of God's own luminous 'ray,' which is the fountain of all light."

Art is revolutionary in a subtle way. Francis of Assisi saw this when he advised: "Do not change the world, change worlds," and Norman O. Brown observed that "art seduces us in the struggle against repression." Art is seductive. Just like beauty. Art is also political. It always has been. To wake people up, to see for oneself what is and behold and then hold that seeing up for others, is a political act. Long ago Plato suggested that to change the music of a culture is to change its mores. During the modern era it was the artists who led the fight to resist the industrialization of our minds, imaginations, and souls. One thinks of William Blake who spoke of the "Divine Imagination," and of poets who critiqued the onslaught of the destruction of the earth. But many modern artists slipped into the role culture gave them, a role of art for art's sake, art for capitalism's sake, art for fame's sake. They forsook the deeper meaning of art, which is art for the community's sake.

Artist and art critic Suzi Gablik has captured the necessary move that artists must make today if they are to grow with the rest of us from a modern to a postmodern era. She says: "Transformation cannot happen from ever-more manic production and consumption in the marketplace; it is more likely to come from some new sense of service to the whole—from a new intensity in personal commitment. . . . The great collective project has, in fact, presented itself. It is that of saving the earth."

Thomas Berry says that we depend on nature's diversity and marvelous beauty to sustain our souls and that to diminish beauty is to diminish the very nurturance of our souls and spirits. We are made to breathe in the intimacy of the rest of nature and its awesome beauty. Without it we cannot survive. "The greatest of human discoveries in the future will be the discovery of human intimacy with all those other modes of being that live with us on this planet, inspire our art and literature, reveal that numinous world whence all things come into being, and with which we exchange the very substance of life." The world is "numinous," he is saying. It is charged with the glory of Divinity itself.

This is an ancient spiritual teaching. It is the teaching of the Cosmic Christ, the glory of God that is found in all things. Hildegard of Bingen put it this way: "The word manifests in every creature." Buddhists call it the "living Buddha" that is manifest in every being.

Seduction is a subtle thing. A gentle thing. Love is its goal. As if to underscore Berry's insistence on the *intimacy* of nature wanting to reveal beauty to us on a regular basis, I woke up this morning to birds singing in the backyard; to roses beckoning in the breeze; to the wind caressing me; to the sea filling my nose with smells and memories of salt air; to fog embracing me with its maternal and wet, gray embrace. Is all this not lessons in intimacy? In closeness and caring? Are we not especially put together for such touchings? Are all our senses not blessed and awakened by such love-making?

To tell these stories anew is to seduce us in the struggle

against repression. It is to let the truth out of the closet: that great things are going on all around us and through us and within us. Things with Divine implications, things that bear the Divine presence and reveal the Divine face. Glory comes alive again. Repression ceases, and oppression takes a backseat.

adam and prometheus, creativity and the christ: is original sin the refusal to create, and is redemption the liberation of creativity?

The reader will recall the story of Prometheus who met with a cruel fate for stealing fire from the gods for the human race. Prometheus stole the fire of the gods and gave it as a gift to the humans who so needed fire to create civilization. When he did this, Zeus was outraged and condemned Prometheus to be lashed to a rock where a vulture would feed each morning on his liver. But his liver grew back again each night. Psychologist Rollo

May interprets the Prometheus story to mean that the artist becomes utterly "beat" after a day's work and is exhausted at night. But during the night, his energy (the liver) grows back again for his work the next day.

I would go further in examining the archetype of the liver. The liver cleanses and recycles. The artist, too, cleanses and recycles the toxins in a culture. Artists turn pain into insight and struggle into triumph and darkness into light and ugliness into beauty and forgetfulness into remembering and grief into rejoicing. Artists add awe to awe and beauty to beauty and wonder to wonder. When the liver is healthy, the person is healthy. The artist is to the community or body politic what the liver is to the human body: a cleanser and recycler of waste and toxins.

REDEMPTION AND ORIGINAL SIN: A REVISIONING

A parallel lesson seems to be told in the Adam and Eve story in the Bible. There, too, human beings are punished for "eating the fruit of the tree of good and evil," that is, for an act of learning and creative consciousness that comes close to Divinity's ways. Says May: "Both the Greek and the Judaeo-Christian myths present creativity and consciousness as being born in rebellion against an omnipotent force."

Now fire is not a luxury—it is practically a necessity for humans, surely for the continuance of our species. So why would the Divine powers be so reluctant to share fire with us? Why should Prometheus have to pay such a dear price for his creativity and his courage? And why should Adam and Eve have to pay such a dear price for eating fruit from the tree of good and evil? Why should we suffer when we create? Why should women give birth in painful labor, and why should artists suffer so deeply in trying to delight and inspire others through their creativity? Was it not a good thing for Prometheus to bend the rules a bit and bring fire to humans? Was it not a good thing for Adam and Eve to have the courage to eat of the tree of good and evil in order to know the difference, to taste the difference? Indeed, since in Hebrew as well as Latin the word for "wisdom" comes from the word for "taste," is the Garden of Eden story not a story about the acquisition of wisdom on the part of our human ancestors? Why should they be punished for acquiring wisdom?

Maybe the answer can be attributed to what the Greeks called the "jealousy of the gods" in the Prometheus story and what the story in Genesis warns regarding the relationship of humans and God: "Ye shall be as gods." Maybe the tasting of good and evil takes us very close—too close for comfort—to our Godly natures. Furthermore, Prometheus is credited not only with giving humans fire but for creating humans in the first place. Our very existence is a challenge to the gods. And to us! Coming face-to-face with the Divine in us makes us feel guilty. And the ultimate punishment for that guilt is death itself (in the Garden of Eden story) or eternal punishment (in the Prometheus story). So much is arrayed *against* our creativity and participation in the wisdom of God, which is the creativity of God: a great guilt, a threat of punishment, and death itself (Adam and Eve).

Saint Augustine said that Adam's sin was an original sin due to pride. I say NO! It was not about pride. It was about *creativity*. Perhaps the original sin, whether in the Prometheus story or the Garden of Eden story, was born of humankind's *need to be creative*. How we respond to this need, this call, this invitation to our Divinity, sets the pace for other generations. One might say we can call the sin "original" because it concerns the way we deal or don't deal with our originality, our creativity. The "original sin" is a haunting fear, a dread of the punishment or wages to be paid, a lurking guilt, at stepping out with our creativity to be counted.

We would prefer to put our imaginations back in the box, to turn our creativity over to others (many of whom are ever so willing to absorb it and dictate to us their own creativity). But then we would feel guilty also. The dilemma for humans is that we are guilty if we create *and* if we choose not to create. Masochism, the desire to turn our power over to others rather than to become empowered and responsible, becomes a popular value in a culture built on such ideologies. So does victimization. The original sin becomes our fear of our own originality, our powers of generativity, our origins, our birth, our genesis, our beginnings—even our *generosity*, which like so much else in the universe is God-like in its scope.

What if the Garden of Eden story is not about our particular peccadilloes but about one sin only—forfeiting our responsibility for creativity, for being co-workers with God? Then redemption means: become a son or daughter of God. Participate in the Divine creativity without guilt and for a purpose that is God-like, namely compassion.

The Christ story picks up on the banishment of Adam and Eve from the Garden of Eden and mystical oneness with God and creation, which is symbolized by that garden. A deep separation haunts our species. Otto Rank talked about the *unio mystica*, our "being at one with the All," and of our deep and ancient yearning to be "in tune with" the cosmos. The opposite is the fullest alienation of all, a feeling of separation from what matters most, separation from the whole, being cut off from the All. In love and art we find a reunion and therefore a healing that is profound and ancient and cosmic. "This identification is the echo of an original identity, not merely of child and mother, but of everything living—witness the reverence of the primitive for animals. In man, identification aims at re-establishing a *lost identity:* Not an identity which was lost once and for all, . . . but *an identity with the cosmic process*, which has to be surrendered and continuously re-established in the course of self-development." Rank calls this loss of cosmic union an "original wound," and I believe this term is far more accurate than the "original sin" term that certain theological traditions have oversold to us. We inherit a wound, not a sin. We *do* sin; we *inherit* wounds.

In Greek, the word for "wound" is "trauma." Is the birth trauma actually due to our unusual physiological situation whereby our heads are almost too big for the birth canal? And, if so, is this not a metaphor for the price we pay for our big brains and our great intellects and their powers for creativity and destruction? We come into the world wounded by our biggest asset—our brains. And whether we rain destruction or love onto others by use of this brain constitutes the story of our life journeys. It is a story addressed by all our spiritual traditions: how to turn woundedness into wisdom.

A wound can be healed, or at least attended to, so its damaging influence is mitigated. The Christ story is a story of the wound being healed. Jesus teaches us to put our "big heads" to the use of compassion and thereby reconnect with the cosmic glory, a union devoutly to be wished. The alienation of being "outside Eden" is healed. Redemption happens. We can pray and act to see that heaven happens on earth.

In the Prometheus story, we are told that his suffering can be alleviated on one condition: that an immortal voluntarily surrender his immortality to come down to help Prometheus out. Hercules is said to have made such a sacrifice to liberate Prometheus. In the Christian story, Paul, in his Letter to the Philippians, tells us that "God became empty of God" in order to join the human race in the person of Jesus and save us from guilt. Was Paul familiar with the Prometheus story? It is hard to believe he was not, since he was educated in Greek and in Hellenistic views of the world. The Cosmic Christ (wisdom incarnate) then becomes the immortal who has voluntarily taken it upon himself in the person of Jesus to join the human species in our dilemma: having the Divine power of creativity, being made in the image and likeness of God, but not being able to exercise it without guilt or fear. *This then is salvation or redemption: liberation to be creative, liberation to exercise our God-given and Divine gifts of creativity.*

But allowing creativity back into our lives is one thing, and using it well is another. We can misuse our creativity. Otto Rank feels this misuse is what got Prometheus in trouble. Prometheus created his love object, Pandora, who, as Prometheus' wish fulfillment, unleashed many evils onto the world. Says Rank: "Here lies the justification for the punishment of Prometheus, whose chaining represents an inhibiting of these presumptuous tendencies in his personality. He is punished not because he steals fire from the gods, fire being after all human property. He is punished because he wants to practice with it the same misuse that apparently was allowed the gods and into which creators of men—parents, educators, or therapists—can so easily fall. This misuse is to impose one's own personality on the creature as so to make it first of all a willing object, and in the future, the successor of one's own ego." The Prometheus complex wants to "dominate creation by means of projection." There is such a thing as creativity without love. Herein lies the danger of creativity. (Is human oppression of nature in today's ecological crisis not an advanced version of this tendency to "dominate creation by means of projection"?)

The Christ story redeems creativity by setting it in the context of compassion. All creativity is meant to serve compassion, not projections. The result of Christ's compassion is a "New Creation" and a new relationship to creation wherein we are reunited with the whole, and all our powers, including our creativity, serve the loving purpose of the whole. In the context of a "universal redemption," we humans are forgiven both for creating and for not creating— though the historical Jesus is very clear that it is best to "bear good fruit" and to increase one's talents and not bury them out of fear and pusillanimity. And the Christ talks also of "bearing fruit that will remain." Thomas Aquinas echoes this teaching when he makes clear that pusillanimity, the fear of our creativity, is a far greater sin than presumption, the willingness to go ahead and create like God. The Christ story reinstates our relationship with the whole, with our original nature, which is indeed to be images and likenesses of the Creator.

The Buddhist tradition offers a parallel teaching on redemption when it promises that through spiritual practice and meditation we can and ought to return to our "original nature," "original mind," or the "universal mind," which is luminous, immaculate, lucid, unstained, and ineffable. This state is called our "Big mind" or "Buddha-Mind." To return to such a state on a regular basis is to become a receptacle for the joy that wants to flow through us to other beings.

This is a creative state. It is a kind of return to our original creativity and our tapping into the creativity that is continuous and unstoppable like "the current of a mighty river."

If creativity is of our origin and if evolution is continuous, then creativity is of our original nature, and when we give birth we give birth to the Buddha nature just as, in the Christian story, we give birth to the Christ when we give birth. Here we tap into the Spirit that desires to co-create with us.

Thus the "original wound" is healed once and for all. We can get on with life—which always means creative life. Redemption becomes that which gives us permission to be creative, compassionate, and God-like. It is that which re-unites us to the All. Rank celebrates the "Divine creative power and Divine knowledge" of Adam from whose side Eve was born, and he compares Adam to Prometheus. Rank, who was not a Christian, nevertheless declares the following: "We recognize therein [in the Prometheus story] the first faint beginnings of that magnificent process of rivaling the Gods, which we have understood psychologically as the gradual acknowledgement of the conscious individual will in the human being. It appears in a glorious fashion in Greek culture with the heroes rebelling against the Gods, and reaches the peak of development in Christianity with the humanizing of God and the deifying of man." Rank has it right: There is a humanizing of God and a deifying of humans in Christianity. And it has to do with the release of creativity.

Evolution moves on as we expand our powers of creative compassion. Prometheus suffered his awful fate for assisting humankind to advance to a next level of evolution—it was not possible to make that advance without fire. Indeed, without fire our species would never have endured this long, for we never would have made it through the ice ages. So Prometheus and the creators of fire-knowledge did a great deed for our species. But they paid a great price. That is our daily experience also: Even when we do good for others we pay a dear price. Consider Martin Luther King, Jr., or Gandhi or Jesus—all were killed for stealing fire, the fire of justice, from the realm of Divinity. The community often does not want to be freed or liberated and projects its sadness, despair, and violence unto those who offer such liberation.

It might be said that, in Rank's view, the "artiste manqué" is the "original sin" of our species. But also, the redemption that Christ brings through Jesus is a redemption from being an "artiste manqué" and returning to our being artists all. Cease being an artiste manqué. Cease your neurosis. Create a culture where creativity is at the center of things, i.e., where Divinity is at the center of things.

Creativity saves. Its opposite kills. The Gospel of Thomas put it this way: "Jesus said: 'When you bring forth that which is within you, that which is yours will save you. But if you do not have that in yourself, that which is not yours in you will kill you.'" Our creativity is a matter of life and death, of salvation and damnation. The stakes are high. Rank felt that the challenge in Deuteronomy—"I put before you life and death—choose life"—was a call to creativity. To choose life means to choose to give birth every day.

WISDOM: THE ARTISAN OF ALL

Wisdom and creativity go together according to our deepest spiritual traditions. Knowledge of itself produces neither creativity nor wisdom. Wisdom has to do with our relationship to the whole, to the cosmos, to nature, to both the feminine and the masculine powers of nature. Wisdom is finding the balance between head and heart, upper chakras and lower chakras, earth and sky, masculine and feminine, joy and sorrow, yin and yang, energy and rest, human and divine, cosmos and psyche.

In the West, the tradition of sacred Wisdom or Sophia finds expression in the Wisdom Tradition of Israel, in the figure of Shekinah, and in the Cosmic Christ. It also took on flesh in the person of the historical Jesus.

In the Hebrew Bible, Wisdom or Sophia is profoundly creative. In Proverbs, she was present at the creation of the world: "Yahweh created me at the beginning of God's work, the first of God's act of long ago. Ages ago I was set up, at the first, before the beginning of the earth." Not only was she present, she was an active participant in creation: "When

God established the heavens, I was there. . . . When God marked out the foundations of the earth, I was beside God as a master worker." Sophia is seen as a "master worker" at the right hand of God the Creator.

In the premodern theology of Thomas Aquinas, wisdom and art go together just as wisdom and nature do. One complements the other. We come to God, who is supreme wisdom, by way of the creatures, who are expressions of that wisdom. The artist comes to the wisdom of God and celebrates it, making it memorable so that we do not miss it. "God is the origin of wisdom." To return to wisdom, then, is to return to our Source. "Wisdom is drawn from God, the first origin, into all creatures that are made through God's wisdom, just as art is drawn from the mind of artists into their work." The Hebrew Scriptures say: "Wisdom pervades and permeates all things" (Wisdom 7:24). This means that every creature contains wisdom and is busy beaming it to us—if we are looking for it and desirous of it. Part of the *intimacy* that we share with the rest of nature is our ability to interact with, dialogue with, even interview other beings about their wisdom. Aquinas puts it this way: "All creatures confess that they are made by God. Human beings ask questions of creatures when they consider them diligently. Those questioned respond. . . ." Reading the book of nature is not that different from reading human books—it all depends on the questions we bring to the project and our willingness to learn. "Just as someone looking at a book knows the wisdom of the writer, so when we see creatures, we know the wisdom of God." This happens because "each creature's beauty is a witness to the Divine Wisdom."

That every creature witnesses to the Divine Wisdom by way of its beauty is an amazing observation. How precious every tree, bush, star, bird, animal, species, person becomes! Imagine that: witnessing to the Divine Wisdom by way of our beauty. How important it must be for every creature to become as beautiful as it can in every way so that it may be the witness it is meant to be to some great, ineffable, mysterious beauty and wisdom. By meditating on the beauty of creation and the wisdom of it we are drawn into transformation ourselves. We learn respect, reverence, wonder, and gratitude. We are changed by the experience. We get in touch with our own wisdom. Then we are ready to be artists ourselves.

What we put into the world contains wisdom also; it, too, is part of the revelation of the Godhead, part of the luminosity that imbues all things. What we put into the world is not cacophony—it does not disrupt the harmony and balance of nature or of psyche. It heals when there is unbalance; it brings equilibrium back when harmony has been lost. It tells the truth when there is cover-up or denial; it ushers in joy when sorrow prevails.

There is art everywhere in the universe; there is wisdom everywhere in the universe. One more reason for psyche and cosmos to come together again—to bring art and wisdom alive once more. As we grow in our appreciation of creation and the whole of it, which we call the "cosmos" (from *kos-mos*, the Greek word for "whole"), we grow in wisdom. And our art will grow in wisdom. That is the exalted promise for a time like ours when so much wisdom is needed and so much new and exciting is being taught us from cosmology. A new cosmology can give birth to a new era of wisdom. That is the promise, the good news, of the times in which we live.

CREATIVITY AND WISDOM IN
THE HISTORICAL JESUS

Among the practitioners of wisdom from our ancestral past was the historical Jesus. It is acknowledged now by the biblical scholars known as the "Jesus Seminar" that the historical Jesus was part of a Wisdom Movement in the first century in Palestine. Scholar Marcus Borg comments that "whatever else can be said about the pre-Easter Jesus, he was a teacher of wisdom—a *sage*, as teachers of wisdom are called." What was that movement? What were its characteristics?

Borg distinguishes two kinds of wisdom teachers—those who reinforce the "ways to live" that a culture has to offer and those who subvert the prevailing wisdom and offer an alternative wisdom. The historical Jesus was of the latter type—he was subversive in his wisdom and offered alternative ways to live out values in his culture. How did he do this? He did it as any artist would do it: by drawing on materials and creating forms that were subversive. That Jesus was an artist of originality and political subversion cannot be denied. His method of choice included aphorisms, or short sayings, and parables, or short stories. Borg puts it this way: "The most certain thing we know about Jesus is that he was a storyteller and speaker of great one-liners." His aphorisms and parables "are the bedrock of the Jesus tradition, and they put us most directly in touch with [his] voice." Jesus was an artist. He brought the Divine Wisdom to bear on his culture and his difficult and dangerous times. His stories and sayings appeal to the imagination in order to confront it and bring about transformation. "They tease the imagination into activity, suggest more than they say, and invite a transformation in perception." Like the prophets of old, Jesus appealed to the imagination by way of the artist he was.

Biblical scholar Walter Brueggemann comments on the relationship between the prophet and the artist when he says: "Every totalitarian regime is frightened of the artist. It is the vocation of the prophet to keep alive the ministry of imagination, to keep on conjuring and proposing alternative futures to the single one the king wants to urge as the only thinkable one." And Thomas Aquinas felt that the proper language of the prophet was always metaphor and symbol. Thus, there are no prophets who are not artists. Maybe this explains why a domineering culture does not see the "value" in educating artists and bringing alive the creativity in all students.

We possess over one hundred of the aphorisms of Jesus today. Among them are the following:

- You cannot serve two masters.
- You cannot get grapes from a bramble bush.
- If a blind person leads a blind person, they will both fall into a ditch.
- Leave the dead to bury the dead.
- You strain out a gnat and swallow a camel. (Borg translation)
- What if those who are the salt must themselves be seasoned?
- Love your enemy.
- Listeners reported: "Your family is outside there looking for you."

    Jesus responded: "My family is inside here looking for God."
- Purity, impurity, and the outside of your cup?

    Purity, impurity, and the inside of your heart!
- To accept the Kingdom is to reject your mother and father.

    To accept the Kingdom is to reject your sisters and brothers.
- No one patches new cloth onto an old garment.

    No one pours new wine into an old wineskin.

    (Crossan translation)

When he creates parables, Jesus is being invitational. He is provoking listeners to think for themselves, as every artist does. Jesus is a "creative storyteller" who gets people to think differently by telling a story like the Good Samaritan or a story like the Prodigal Son. As Borg puts it, in the parables "the appeal is not to the will—not 'Do this'—but rather 'Consider seeing it this way.' As invitational forms of speech, the parables do not invoke external authority. . . . Rather, their authority rests in themselves—that is, in their ability to involve and affect the imagination." For all artists, the authority resides within the work itself and not outside in some external authority. It comes from within and speaks to the within. Jesus as artist was no different in this respect. Borg does not minimize the radicalness of Jesus' chosen art form. Jesus' work invites "his hearers to see in a radically new way. The appeal is to the imagination. . . . This emphasis upon *seeing* runs throughout his message. There are those who have eyes and yet do not see." Jesus is trying to awaken us. Like Buddha did. Like all artists must.

To get us to see another way is to reject the conventional way of seeing, to subvert the ordinary way of seeing and judging in one's culture. Jesus stood against much of the consciousness of his culture. Borg says he "directly attacked the central values of his social world's conventional wisdom: family, wealth, honor, purity, and religiosity." He also critiqued images of God that his culture and religion took for granted, images of God as judge and lawgiver versus images of God as generous and compassionate and a lover of all of nature's beings and all the beauty contained therein:

"Consider the birds of the air—they neither sow nor reap, they have neither storehouse nor barn, and yet God feeds them.

"Consider the lilies of the field, how they grow; they neither toil nor spin, yet I tell you, even Solomon in all his glory was not arrayed like one of these."

Yet death comes to the flowers as it does to all things. "But if God so clothes the grass of the field, which today is alive and tomorrow is thrown into the oven, how much more will he clothe you?" Jesus is drawing wisdom from the world around him and arousing it in his listeners.

In the Prodigal Son parable we see what Borg calls "Jesus' artistry as a storyteller, his invitational style, his subversion of conventional wisdom, and the ground of his alternative wisdom—namely, an image of God as gracious and compassionate." Borg feels that it was Jesus' emphasis on the *heart* and on the need for a *new heart* that lay at the core of his invitations to see the world differently and with an alternative wisdom. Jesus speaks from his own heart, from his own experience. "As one who knew God, Jesus knew God as the compassionate one, not as the God of requirements and boundaries." Central to Jesus' teaching is an invitation to *behold* God by experiencing God. "That change—from having heard about God with the hearing of the ear to 'beholding' God, from secondhand belief to firsthand relationship—is what the alternative wisdom of Jesus is most centrally about." As we have seen above, the artist beholds what is and holds it up for the rest of us to see better. Jesus did no less.

Jesus Seminar scholar John Dominic Crossan comments on the words from Jesus' mouth: "Blessed are the destitute."

This is not a romantic invocation of the homeless but a well thought out critique of power structures. "Jesus speaks to a situation of systemic injustice and structural evil, where empires live off colonies, aristocrats live off peasants, and only a large percentage of expendable people make the process possible." In this context, "only those expendables are blessed, only the destitute are innocent. A contemporary version might read: 'Only the homeless are blameless.'"

Crossan sees another strategy in the wisdom of Jesus besides his aphorisms and parable stories that get people to see differently. That is the strategy of getting persons of different classes and social ranks to dine together. This *meal strategy* was meant to get people mixing, to mix up the stratified social structures that so often go unnoticed and that perpetuate injustice. Behind this strategy there lies a trust in human nature: As people mix and hear one another's stories, there will be less violence and more understanding, less division and more community. Healing will take place, or at least is possible to take place. The "table was and is a miniature model for society," Crossan believes.

Still another strategy from the historical Jesus was that of healing. Jesus was a healer. He offered people hope of relief from some of their deepest pains—psychological and political as well as physical. Says Crossan: "The Kingdom movement was Jesus' program of empowerment for a peasantry becoming steadily more hard-pressed through insistent taxation, attendant indebtedness, and eventual land expropriation, all within increasing commercialization in the expanding colonial economy of a Roman Empire."

How did the wisdom of Jesus assert itself in those trying circumstances? "Jesus *lived* against the systemic injustice and structural evil of that situation, an alternative open to all who would accept it: a life of open healing and shared eating, of radical itinerancy, programmatic homelessness, and fundamental egalitarianism, of human contact without discrimination, and of Divine contact without hierarchy. He also died for that alternative." Thus Crossan sees Jesus' activities as addressing healing of the socioeconomic kind (eating) and the religio-political kind (healing). Both were radical, both were subversive, both led to his early death.

Wisdom disturbs. She is "a friend of the prophets" and associates with those who must offer alternatives to the dominant cultural values. The historical Jesus was such a person. Wisdom heals, saves, and preserves. Sophia, or Wisdom's role in Israel, was understood to be, in Borg's words, "essentially prophetic. Though a Wisdom figure, she speaks very much like the classical prophets of ancient Israel: in the marketplaces and public squares, she calls to people to heed her words and warns of calamity and disaster to befall those who ignore her counsel." Thus, her role and that of the historical Jesus are seen to overlap.

CREATIVITY AMONG
THE EARLIEST CHRISTIANS

Didn't Jesus' reference to being wisdom give permission to others, indeed to all of us, to be wisdom ourselves, "playing with God before the creation of the world"? Play and co-creation are ours now just as they were for Jesus. Wisdom is at hand—our hands. Isn't this the meaning of empowerment? Isn't this, in turn, the full meaning and message of redemption? Redemption remains ambiguous; it is never fully done; it depends on our choices and our deeds right up to the end of our lives. Redemption is ambiguous as creativity is ambiguous. The question: "Who is saved?" is changed to: "Who is saving?" What are we doing to awaken from the dead, to give birth, to heal and make alive again? What are we doing to birth compassion?

Like Wisdom, we are also invited to approach life from a cosmic perspective. Wisdom is transnational and trans-human. She cares about "all" of God's creation. The power of Wisdom loves all of creation. We are called to do the same. This attitude is also redemptive; it rescues us from the ills that accompany anthropocentrism. It makes our souls big again, growing with delight and joy. Such joy heals. Compassion happens. Our species evolves into what it is capable of—becoming instruments of Divine compassion.

The earliest Christian writers and storytellers took their creative work seriously. Burton Mack has said that what birthed Christianity was an "explosion of imagination" combined with a "group experimenting with a new social vision." The work of the historical Jesus was *empowerment*—"communal empowerment," as Crossan emphasizes. Jesus, by his originality and courage, set in motion the originality and courage of many others. He called on his followers to imitate his example. And sometimes they did.

The gospels themselves, we are learning more and more, are full of imagination. They are full of Jesus' followers putting words into his mouth. Indeed, it is estimated that 80 to 85 percent of the gospels are of this kind—not words straight from the historical Jesus but words that later writers put into his mouth.

Is this a scandal? By no means. The early writers were not modern historians nor were they striving to be. They were excited witnesses of those who had heard Jesus speak or had heard the stories of those who had. Things got embellished; things got retold; stories grew; different authors were adapting the stories to different audiences and different ideologies. The bottom line is this: *The gospels were put together by amazing artists and even amazing poets. We have underestimated once again the power of the artists, the leadership of the artists, and in this case the teachers (more than scribes or theologians) of the church, who are the gospel-makers.* The gospel-makers were imitating the historical Jesus, at least in this respect: They were being creative. And in doing so they put together stories, texts, and sayings that have nourished hearts and souls for two thousand years.

How creative were these writers? Crossan talks about the "tremendous creative freedom of one gospel writer in using another and especially in dealing with the words and deeds of Jesus himself." He talks of the "act of religious genius" that combined two streams of tradition into a "creative interaction with each other" when it came to weaving the "fulfillment" and "prophecy" stories of the Hebrew Bible into a coherent story in conjunction with the death of Jesus. Passion prophecy, then passion narrative, and finally an interaction between the two emerged at the hands of highly skilled artists whom we call gospel writers.

Philosopher Thomas Sheehan talks of the "genius" of the pre-Marcan storytellers who essentially left the question about the empty tomb open. He calls the story "a gem of storytelling which brilliantly subverts its own apparent theme." It becomes "one of the richest parables about the Kingdom of God-with-man to be found in the Christian repertoire. Like all parables, it confronts the listener with a question and a decision. . . . It hinges on surprise and the reversal of expectations." One might say that these early writers were very much following in the spirit of their master who was a brilliant parable-maker. The Easter account, as it evolved, included making up a story of an apocalyptic angel who recited the resurrection formula to the women who had originally found the tomb empty.

The bottom line is that the story *did evolve.* It grew—creativity grew it. One might say the power of the Spirit unleashed by the Cosmic Christ grew it. It seems that we are just beginning to realize the immense contribution that artists made to the earliest decades of the Christian story.

They were not historians as we understand historians, but they were artists as we understand artists. They made it all interesting, amazing, and memorable. They wrote parables as their master, Jesus, spoke them. Indeed, Crossan believes that Christianity owes its survival to the artists who composed these writings: "Jesus' Kingdom movement among the illiterate peasant class could have died out within one or two generations as a local or regional phenomena had not literate leadership from at least the lower echelons of the scribal or retainer class been also early at work." These literate writers read the sources and created the stories that carried the power of the narrative in a convincing manner.

THE COSMIC CHRIST, THE HISTORICAL JESUS, AND WISDOM'S CREATIVITY

The earliest Christian hymns and some of the earliest writings we possess (namely, Paul's epistles) are born of a great imagination and creativity. Indeed, the imagination is on a *cosmic scale*. For the message derived from much of the Christian writings of the first century is not only that Jesus *taught* wisdom but that Jesus *was Wisdom*. The development of Christology was clearly an imaginative development, one that went on in the imaginations of his followers long before the institutional church inherited the empire in the fourth century (a dubious accomplishment, indeed). There began a movement that saw Jesus as "intimately related to the wisdom of God" (Borg). This movement grew, and it represented the earliest development of an understanding of Jesus' relationship to God. It was older than calling Jesus "Son of God," which came later.

The early Christians applied the Wisdom motif to Jesus or, better, to the Christ in Jesus. The Logos was present from the beginning of time assisting God in creation. This is surely an embellishment. "The Hellenistic Jewish Christians adapted and enhanced the Jewish Wisdom myth to fit the needs of their mission to the Gentiles," notes scholar Thomas Sheehan. This was another creative act on the part of the writers of the early Christian texts.

The historical Jesus who got himself crucified was not aware of such awesome lineage—*or was he?* Perhaps he was. Perhaps he really did come to proclaim to all the people, and especially the downtrodden, that we are all sons and daughters of wisdom, all present at the beginning of the world, all master workers at God's sides, co-workers with God and Spirit. Perhaps the early Christian writers, while surely going beyond the literal words of the historical Jesus, were indeed being true to a spirit that he unleashed: the spirit of trusting in the Spirit and participating with the Creator in creative acts of co-creation.

As the theology of Sophia developed in Judaism, she came to take on "qualities and functions normally attributed to God," as Borg puts it. Sophia becomes "the fashioner of all things" and the "mother" of all good things who "pervades and penetrates all things." She also "renews all things." And she comes to us all (not just to the historical Jesus!), for "in every generation, she passes into holy souls." Thus she becomes our co-worker when we give birth; the work of creation gets carried on as co-creation between ourselves and Sophia, ourselves and Spirit. It is not so strange, then, that persons writing of Jesus and coming from this same Jewish tradition also evolved their thinking as they saw Jesus gradually move from teacher to personification of Wisdom, to a Wisdom that was like God.

Some of the earliest sources of the historical Jesus connect him to Sophia and imply that he saw himself as Sophia. Luke, expressing a Q passage (dating from the early 50s), says: "The Sophia of God said. . . ." (Luke 11:49) when he is referring to Jesus. Luke reports Jesus saying: "Yet Sophia is vindicated by her children" (Luke 7:35; cf. Matthew 11:19). Borg comments: "Taken together, these two passages imply that the early Christian movement saw Jesus as both the spokesperson and the child of Sophia, and that Jesus himself may have spoken of himself in these terms."

The Q Gospel and the Gospel of Thomas (dating from between the 50s and the 70s C.E.) both emphasize Jesus' sayings over his deeds. Both are emphasizing Jesus as Wisdom's voice. Crossan concludes that this tradition must date "at least from the 40s. It is, in other words, a very early stream of Christian tradition." Crossan sees Wisdom from the Hebrew Bible tradition lying behind both saying collections and passion narratives.

The Gospel of Thomas pictures Jesus addressing the importance of creativity in our lives on several occasions. He says: "The Kingdom is in your center and is about you. When you know your Selves, then you will be known, and you will be aware that you are the sons of the Living Father." Isn't the creative act that process by which we come to terms with our "center"? And isn't getting to know ourselves part of the creative act and that which makes us "sons of the Living Father"? And again: "The disciples said to him: 'Tell us in what way our end will be.' Jesus said: 'Have you therefore discerned the beginning in order that you seek after the end? For in the place where the beginning is, there will be the end. Happy is he who will stand boldly at the beginning. He shall know the end and will not taste death.'" Part of the creative process is to return to the beginning, to become childlike again, vulnerable to awe and wonder. The creative process requires courage or "standing boldly at the beginning." Death will not overcome the creative person who is leaving behind a gift.

Jesus urges people to tell the world what they experience deep inside: "What you will hear in one ear and in the other ear, that proclaim from your housetops. For no one lights a lamp and puts it under a bowl, nor does he put it in a hidden place, but he sets it on the lamp stand in order that everyone who goes in and comes out may see its light." This passage surely captures the drivenness of the artist to tell the world what he or she has seen, felt, heard deep inside.

Jesus equates the work of the human to that of fruit trees. "A good man brings forth good from his storehouse, a bad man brings forth ill from his wicked storehouse which is in his heart, and he speaks ill: for out of the abundance of the heart he brings forth ill." The heart is the place from which we draw our fruit, be it a good heart bearing good fruit or a bad heart bearing ill fruit. It is from the heart that we derive our creativity ultimately, as an ancient Mesoamerican poem put it: "The true artist draws out all from his heart. . . . God is in his heart. He puts divinity into things."

Paul speaks of Jesus as the Sophia of God even as he proposes his own version of conventional wisdom versus alternative wisdom. For Paul, conventional wisdom is living "under the law," and alternative wisdom is "living by grace." Paul also reproduces early Christian hymns that sing of the preexistence of Christ "through whom are all things and through whom we exist" (I Corinthians). "All things have been created through him and for him. He himself is before all things, and in him all things hold together" (Colossians 1:16). Thus, as early as Paul, writing in the 50s, Jesus becomes the embodiment of Sophia. Another name for this is the Cosmic Christ.

In the prologue to John's Gospel, Sophia is spoken about when the Logos is named. "In the beginning was Sophia," and "Sophia became flesh and dwelt among us." Jesus thus becomes the incarnation of Divine Sophia, Sophia made flesh. John's whole gospel is a gospel of Wisdom incarnate.

Thus Sophia constitutes "the earliest Christology of the Christian movement," according to Borg. It is also widespread, found, as we have seen, in the synoptics, Paul and John.

To say that Sophia is central to the earliest Christian message and to the work of the historical Jesus is to say that creativity is central to the earliest Christian message and to the work of the historical Jesus. Furthermore, Sophia is the bridge to the Cosmic Christ and to the earliest development of Christology. That is to say, creativity and cosmology are central to the earliest development of Christology. Why have we not heard this before? Perhaps because fourth-century Christology took another path— that of proving that Jesus was "the only son of God"—a path that buttressed an empire but that failed to carry on the Spirit and message of the historical Jesus and of the Cosmic Christ.

Medieval theology understood the Spirit of the Cosmic Christ, its relation to wisdom and to our creativity. Thus Hildegard of Bingen writes:

> *God's word is in all creation, visible and invisible.*
> *The Word is living, being, spirit, all verdant greening, all creativity.*
> *The Word manifests in every creature.*

Meister Eckhart sees us all as "mothers of God" who give birth whenever we give birth to nothing less than the Christ, the son and daughter of God. We birth ourselves also as other Christs. "Not only is the Son of the heavenly Creator born in this darkness—but you too are born there as a child of the same heavenly Creator and none other." Indeed, all creatures participate in the creativity of the Divine Word or Cosmic Wisdom, for "God has poured the Divine image and likeness in all creatures."

We have come a long way from the guilt of Prometheus and Adam and Eve. This is redemption: that we be creative like God is. And that our creativity and co-creation serve God's agenda, which is always compassion.

revisioning easter and pentecost: rolling away the obstacles to creativity so that the spirit of creativity can resurrect

What happens when we apply the essence of our humanity, namely our creativity, to the Easter story? Once the fear of death—a major obstacle to creativity—is removed, can we then be free to embark on our true destiny, which is to create. To create like God does. To create for compassion's sake and celebration's sake and healing's sake and joy's sake.

Is it also possible that the terror that death and the possibility of non-existence bring to us can also goad us into creating, into going to the edge where we encounter depths of ourselves that we did not know were ours to give?

EASTER: OVERCOMING
THE FEAR OF DEATH

Death threatened both Adam and Eve and Prometheus for their daring to be creative. The Easter story addresses the threat of death. Death is destroyed. Nothing more to fear there. The threats against our creativity are neutralized by the resurrection event. Now we can get on with being who we are, co-creators, sons and daughters of the Divine Creator. And here lies redemption.

Paradise means "garden." Being driven from the garden, as Adam and Eve were, is being banished from paradise or heaven, a heaven on earth. (Jesus teaches people to pray that things might occur on earth as they do in heaven.) Good Friday began in the garden of Gethsemane where betrayal occurred and where soldiers came to capture Jesus. The Easter story is about recovering paradise, finding the fullness of delight and Sabbath, resurrecting from death and the fear of death. Easter happens in a garden, and in one version the risen Christ is encountered as a gardener. The Song of Songs, like the Easter stories so full of garden imagery, redeems the lost Garden of Eden as well. Death is the ultimate in non-communication (remember that "hell" means "concealment"). Death is the ultimate in *no creativity*. For all creativity is communication; it is the utmost in communication, the telling of our story, our hearts, our truth, our inner wisdom, our search for beauty, and our telling of pain.

Easter is about paradise restored—communication and

creativity come alive. The Easter story is about the triumph of creativity. What is wilder in its implications, wilder in its revolutionary imagination, than the notion that resurrection overcomes death? Otto Rank has called the resurrection story the "most revolutionary idea" that humans have yet to come up with. In the Easter story, a "large boulder" blocks the door to the tomb where Jesus' body lies. We are all entombed with large boulders blocking our escape and liberation to the extent that our creativity is blocked or stifled. "Who will roll away the stone from the tomb?" the women asked on their way to the tomb on Easter morning, prepared as they were to anoint the body of Jesus. The answer came soon enough. An angel did it. "The angel of the Lord, descending from heaven, came and rolled away the stone and sat on it" (Matthew 28:1).

We need to remove the obstacles and roll away the stones for the very natural powers of creativity to emerge again. If this is so, surely it helps to name the obstacles, to identify the stones that inhibit our creativity. In this way we will know and recognize the angels of any stripe who are coming to assist us. And come they surely shall. For angels come when humans are in trouble. What better time, then, for the angels' arrival than now?

ROLLING AWAY THE OBSTACLES TO CREATIVITY

At a recent retreat conducted by mystical author Andrew Harvey and myself, we asked the participants the following question: "What are the principal obstacles to your creativity?" The answers were both practical and profound, and they amount to a naming of the boulders that need rolling back from the tomb if we are to resurrect our spirits and *the* Spirit of Creativity, the Holy Spirit. Indeed, so deep and provocative are the replies that this exercise reveals to me the question we dealt with in chapter 2 of this book: how central creativity is to our very nature as human beings. For to inquire about what prevents our creativity, it turns out, *is to reveal the essence of who we are and who we are becoming or failing to become.*

Among the answers offered by the participants were the following:

1. The fear of Bigness—mine and God's—that I might encounter if I really let my creativity express itself.
2. The fear of my homosexuality—the harassment I would receive (even greater than I now receive) if I were truly honest about who I am sexually and how that would emerge through my creativity.
3. My lack of feeling, my lack of spiritual depth.
4. Sadness. Sadness prevents my being spontaneous and creative.

5. The difficulty of surrendering and the price I would have to pay for doing so.
6. My early exposure to teachers who taught me to squelch my passion and my enthusiasm when I was a child.
7. Fear of death.
8. A need to control and put control first.
9. Identification with failure.
10. Lack of money and financial resources.
11. Fear of loss of identity.
12. Shyness.
13. Acceptance and surrender to the great physical pain I have been in for years.
14. Scared of my heart cracking open.
15. Victimization as a child that taught me to give my power to others. I was very creative as a child, but my mother "squelched me like a bug—and still does."
16. Fear of abandonment.
17. My very busy mind.
18. Too narrow an understanding of "artist" or "creativity"—as if we are not all blessed with creative powers and choices every moment of our lives.
19. Workaholism.
20. Being a white, male, heterosexual and not knowing what my creative agenda ought to be (my gay, lesbian, black, and feminist friends all seem to know what their community requires of them).

21. A lack of faith that Spirit can prevail and work through us.

22. Too many administrative responsibilities.

23. Too little free time and too little money to "buy" that free time.

24. Lack of community support. I am considered odd for being so creative and that is okay, but it would be nice if I had that support.

25. Second-guessing myself; fear of failure and rejection and the notion that I might have to give up my comforts; the demands that would be made on my lifestyle if I truly committed to my creativity.

26. Fear of being alone, of rocking the boat and making people uncomfortable; people would then abandon me; shame.

27. Despair can be overwhelming. What difference can I make? Will it last? Inertia and distractions brought on by a middle-class lifestyle.

28. Perfectionism. Taking the time to be creative.

What is resurrection? Resurrection is the rolling away of these boulder-sized obstacles from our hearts and minds in order that the natural process of creativity might emerge.

The late M. C. Richards once wrote: "We have to realize that a creative being lives within ourselves, whether we like it or not, and that we must get out of its way, for it will give us no peace until we do." What if creativity were totally natural? What if M. C. Richards were exactly correct and our duty is to "get out of its way" or we will never find peace? What if creativity were so built into the forces of the universe that we could never join the universe, never connect psyche and cosmos, unless and until we surrendered to creativity in our lives and relationships?

Isn't this what the New Creation story is telling us? That creativity is everywhere, that it is the *longest-standing habit of the universe*? Why, then, aren't we more active in pursuing creativity and teaching it and calling this teaching "education"?

Our universities have sucked the universe out of the university for the most part. We resist the teaching of cosmology. Maybe we do this because we resist releasing the powers of creativity. Maybe we—and our institutions—are terrified of the universe still and, like Descartes, prefer fear to risk. (Recall that it was Descartes's disillusionment with life because of the sudden death of the king of France—whom he so admired when he was a young man—that fed his philosophy, which was in so many ways a philosophy of control.) What we are most terrified of is the hint of death that is behind every creative act.

Otto Rank, who spent his life counseling great artists, including Anaïs Nin and Henry Miller, defines the artist in terms of death when he says: "The artist is one who wants to leave behind a gift." "Leave behind," he says. Why does he say that? The artist is leaving us, is exiting, *and knows it.* The artist is not in denial about death. Furthermore, the artist is not exiting quietly. No, the artist is leaving us with a memory, a memorial, a painting or a song or a symphony or a poem or a dance or an insight—and not just any memory, memorial, painting, song, symphony, poem, dance, or insight—but one that can be recognized *as a gift*. There is a blessing to this left-behind thing; there is a goodness to it; it is a gift, not a curse; it is a gift, not a neutral thing. And why a "gift"? Why do we deserve a gift from every artist who leaves us? Well, it is not what we deserve. It is not a gift *to us*, though it is a gift *for us*. The gift is to life itself. The gift is a thank you to life. The gift is to the life-giver, and, as Rank dares to say, the gift is always to God.

Both the Prometheus story and the Adam and Eve story connect the "stealing of the Divine creativity" with death. In this context, the resurrection story of Christianity becomes an affirmation of our creativity, an act of permission to carry on our Divine likeness without guilt and without fear. Not even the fear of death. We are now free to live, i.e., to create.

This is how Rollo May puts it, borrowing from Otto Rank: "Creativity is a yearning for immortality. . . . Creativity comes from this struggle—out of the rebellion the creative act is born. Creativity is born of a great passion—the passion of the adult human being, which is a passion to live beyond one's death." May believes that the passion of the artist is born of the resistance to death of all kinds. The artist requires "an intensity of emotion, a heightened vitality—for is not the vital forever in opposition to death? . . . The rage is against injustice. . . . But ultimately it is rage against the prototype of all injustice—death."

This is why Otto Rank called the resurrection story the

most "revolutionary idea" that humans have yet to come up with, for it democratizes immortality, and in doing so it democratizes creativity. No longer does any human have to fear the retribution of the gods (or of God) for tapping into the Divine creativity. Quite the opposite: We are now encouraged to be as fruitful as the Creator, as fruitful as Mary, to bring the "Christ" (or the Buddha) into the world, into our beings, personalities, work, and citizenship.

Another link between creativity and death is that when we create we are disturbing the peace (including the pseudo-peace that so often reigns). To disturb the pseudo-peace—which always benefits a few—is to make enemies, often enemies in powerful places, enemies with the power to kill or to destroy. Otto Rank did this in defying his mentor, Sigmund Freud. Rank, who was the youngest and most brilliant of Freud's early followers, left the circle when Freud committed what Rank believed was reductionism on the artist. In his book on Leonardo da Vinci, Freud proposed that all Da Vinci's genius came from his mother complex. When Rank exited Freud's circle, he was vilified, effectively wiped off the books, by his Freudian brothers. Indeed, his name and work have in great part been forgotten by the "death" that was pronounced against him for upsetting the orthodoxy of the Freudian inner circle.

Other examples abound. Jesus is an obvious one. A creative preacher-prophet who got himself killed. Not an altogether unfamiliar story in the history of the prophets, those who live by their social imaginations and dare to try to get the rest of us to live fully. Mahatma Gandhi and Martin Luther King, Jr., follow this trend.

It would seem, then, that the ancient myths of Prometheus and Adam and Eve are not just idle stories. They are true stories; they tell the truth about the hatred that is awakened when creativity happens and is let loose in a society that resists justice. Once again, the Christ story is a powerful one, for it encourages the artist in us *to put life first and not to fear the forces of death*. For even if the forces of death prevail (as they did on Good Friday), still they will not succeed in the long run (for there is an Easter Sunday). That the historical Jesus met the fate of so many creative people is not so surprising; that his life and death and resurrection have inspired others, such as King and Gandhi, to risk life and limb in the cause of the Divine creativity bent on justice is an apt response to his memory.

Goethe summarized the relationship between art, death, and the spiritual journey when he wrote:

> *I praise what is truly alive,*
> *What longs to be burned to death.*

> *In the calm water of the love-nights,*
> *Where you were begotten, where you have begotten,*
> *A strange feeling comes over you*
> *When you see the silent candle burning. . . .*

And as long as you haven't experienced
This to die and so to grow
You are only a troubled guest
On the dark earth.

To create is to die, and it is to bring being into the world that can and will die. (Yet to create is also to live beyond death and to touch immortality, as we have seen above.) To create is to open the doors to death but to do so willingly and knowingly. Perhaps this is the warning that Prometheus, Adam and Eve, and Jesus extend to us who desire to be creative. One does pay a price for this fire. Consider the mother whose child dies young. Consider St. Francis whose Franciscan order was snatched from him before he even died. Grief is real. The artist is, one might say, asking for it. The artist draws the fire of creativity and thereby tempts death itself. Failure. Poverty. Isolation. But the artist has realized that the alternative to creativity is worse than death. It is boredom. A death of the Spirit. A soul-death. A concealment of one's truth. Hell.

GRACE OVER GUILT: PENTECOST, THE COMING OF THE HOLY SPIRIT OF CREATIVITY

Pentecost is the occasion for the sending of the Spirit. What spirit? The Spirit of Creativity and co-creation, the Spirit of truth, therefore, that the Christ promised in John's Gospel. "I still have many things to say to you, but they would be too much for you now. But when the Spirit of truth comes he will lead you to the complete truth" (John 16:12–13). This Spirit of truth heals the Tower of Babel and speaks in tongues that unite nations and disparate tribes instead of dividing them as Babel did. The coming of the Holy Spirit—our creativity come alive. Inspired. On fire. Burning. A burning bush in our times, burning imaginations connected to a burning heart meant to renew and redeem. The prophet Joel was invoked on the first Pentecost day in a sermon preached by Peter. Joel promised that "your old ones shall see visions and your young ones shall dream dreams." The occasion, as Peter saw it, was the coming of the Spirit to *all* humankind. We are all now touched by the Creative Spirit. We cannot run from it or deny it. It is our destiny as a species.

The key to understanding Pentecost is that the coming of the Holy Spirit is a grace and not a work, that the Spirit of Creativity pursues us; we don't manufacture it. This is where the Jewish and Christian traditions surpass the Prometheus story: Prometheus had to *steal* the Divine fire for humans; the Christian and Jewish God *is giving it away!* That is what "grace" is: a give-away. Our job is to be ready and receptive. Then the Spirit cannot help but come.

If creativity is a grace and not a work (though it requires our work to put it into practice), then *guilt is banished*. For it is not our doing. Pentecost moves us beyond relationships of guilt and therefore of shame. The Spirit comes; we respond. Get on with it. Get the job done. Solve problems. Sans guilt.

Creativity challenges head-on the issue of guilt. Part of both the Prometheus story and the Adam and Eve story is the guilt associated with breaking new ground. God's laws set us up for this guilt. Rollo May comments that "creativity provokes the jealousy of the gods. This is why authentic creativity takes so much courage: an active battle with the gods is occurring." In the Bible, the second of the Ten Commandments tells us to avoid making graven images: "But the commandment also expresses the timeless fear that every society harbors of its artists, poets, and saints. For they are the ones who threaten the status quo, which each society is devoted to protecting." Thus guilt accompanies creativity. "Creativity carries such an inexplicable guilt feeling," observes May. So many artists and poets commit suicide, and often at the very height of their achievement. Others fall into addictions of alcohol and drugs that come close to self-destruction.

In this sense, the Christ event in Jesus is redemptive. The "guilt" that is being expiated is not so much the guilt for our daily peccadilloes as it is the guilt for our *daring to be creative, our daring to be Divine.* Jesus was one who suffered death in great part because of jealousy and envy. His creativity was too much—it was challenging the powers that be, *and* it was awakening others to challenge the same powers. If he had had no followers, the story might have ended differently. But in killing Jesus something happened to his followers. They eventually became more strengthened in their resolve to attempt to imitate his disobedience, that is, to emulate his creativity. So much so that Paul could exclaim that "it is no longer I who live but Christ who lives within me." What does an empire do with citizens like that? What does an empire do with a movement like that, one that substitutes one person willing to die for his moral imagination with still another and another and another? We know what the empire did. It killed Paul. And Peter. And thousands of others in bloody spectacle. But eventually it succumbed. Imagination won out. Resurrection won out. The Divine Creativity won out *and* its expiation of human guilt for being God-like, i.e., for being creative and taking responsibility for one's creativity.

When Ernest Becker says "better guilt than responsibility," he is reminding us of what our options in this life are. If we follow the path of guilt, we are abandoning the path of responsibility. Guilt can so wrap us up and tie us in knots that all our energy and imagination are fed into our "guilt trips," and there is nothing left for other kinds of trips. But if we choose responsibility, which is our creativity, then we overcome guilt.

`We need to choose, Becker is saying, between responsibility and guilt. We have some wonderful models, of whom the historical Jesus is one: Imagine the doubt he must have experienced in siding with his imagination against his religious culture and the Roman Empire at once. Yet what confidence he had in the God he had encountered, who not only sustained him but drew out of him his own sense of responsibility. Jesus did not succumb to guilt. He followed his vocation instead. In this sense, too, his death is redemptive, that is to say, it frees us from guilt and toward responsibility, but only if we grasp his story in its fullness and in light of the Divine imperative to create as God does.

EMBRACING SOLITUDE
AND ALONENESS

To be creative one must learn to be at home with solitude or healthy aloneness. Loneliness, solitude, and separation from the community accompany creativity. Of course the artist is lonely—intellectually alone and often morally alone. After all, he or she is bringing something *new* into the world.

The *Tao Te Ching* instructs us as follows:

> *Ordinary men hate solitude.*
> *But the Master makes use of it,*
> *Embracing his aloneness, realizing*
> *He is one with the whole universe.*

When it comes to our creativity, we all move beyond being "ordinary men and women." We are called to embrace solitude.

When Picasso painted his *Les demoiselles d'Avignon* in 1907, it created such a stir among friends and foes alike that he did not display it publicly for several years. This painting, today considered a masterpiece and a turning point in the history of art, brought fierce opposition down on Picasso. He comments on the importance of taking risks: "Painting is freedom. If you jump, you might fall on the wrong side of the rope. But if you are not willing to take the risk of breaking your neck, what good is it? You don't jump at all. You have to wake people up. To revolutionize their way of identifying things. You've got to create images they won't accept." Only two dealers showed interest in Picasso's work, and one of them commented: "What I'd like to make you realize at once is the incredible heroism of a man like Picasso, whose moral loneliness was, at the time, quite horrifying, for none of his painter friends had followed him. Everyone found that picture crazy or monstrous."

The story is told of Martin Luther King Junior's bringing a proposition to his board of twenty-two persons. The proposition was about his coming out publicly against the Vietnam War. The board was adamantly against it. They had enough troubles already. Their financial situation was tottering. They did not need another huge controversy to add to the other issues they were wrestling with and the other fires they were trying to contain. At the board meeting the vote was twenty-one to one *not* to come out against the war. The next day Dr. King held a press conference in which he announced his opposition to the war.

Was King alone? Of course he was. Every prophet at times is very alone. And every artist. And that is okay. The artist has to learn to be at home with his or her inner voice, with God, with the Source of all imagination and ethics and life itself. This aloneness is not the same as "being a loner" (although sometimes one will be accused of this by one's community). Rather, it is about being with one's conscience and learning to listen to newer drums. How can one do this if one is involved in idle chatter with the prevalent mores of the crowds around one? One has to learn to act alone at times and to listen to the powers that will sustain one.

I know a painter who paints behind locked doors because he says he does not want anyone mocking him. You see, he talks to the canvas and to the spirits that emerge from the canvas, and from this his paintings are born. But they require solitude, these spirits, to emerge. And they require his full focus. People love his paintings and he loves people and he loves to share his paintings. But they do not come, cannot come, merely from being among the people or hanging out with them. They come from an act of deliberate seclusion, an act of solitude freely chosen.

One wonders if this is not reason enough for every artist and the artist in every one of us to learn to meditate. Meditation teaches us not to fear being alone. In meditation we learn to calm the mind and its infinite powers of distraction and projection so that stillness might be entertained on a regular basis. With the stillness comes Spirit. Silence gives way for Spirit to arrive. The Quakers know this, and all who meditate know this. Stillness gives way to centeredness. I once met a plastic surgeon who told me he gets up at four o'clock every morning in order to spend two hours in meditation before going to work. "If I didn't do this," he said, "I would succumb to my success, and life for me would be nothing but the fancy money I make and the things it would buy." Maybe this is why Otto Rank says that success is the greatest enemy of the artist. If we succeed and have not prepared our soul for success by teaching it to honor solitude, then we may be in trouble. So many artists do get themselves in trouble. When success is not balanced with solitude, fame can snatch away one's soul, it can seize one just as much as any other addiction. It can dictate to the soul and kill the soul. Meditation nurtures the soul with good food, with the food of silence and aloneness.

After all, much of the price of success is fame, and much of fame is projection. Consider the film clips we see of teenagers idolizing pop stars from Frank Sinatra to Elvis Presley, from the Beatles to the Grateful Dead. If the players took this adolescent projection seriously, they would die from it all. Some of them have. For the soul was not made for someone else's projections, whether negative ("let us kill the bastard") or positive ("oh, I'm so in love with you"). Both projections are deadly. The artist, like all of us, must become so at home with oneself and with the truth of one's own being that he or she is not pushed to the breaking point by others' projections. Sometimes it may be easier to endure negative projections (anger can take over to protect us) than positive ones.

Otto Rank carries the subject of fame, adulation, and

projection even deeper when he explains that all neurosis derives from the artiste manqué. In other words, there are very many people walking around (especially in our couchpotatoitis-ridden consumer culture today) who have not developed the artist in them. This is a disaster. It is, in Rank's opinion, the cause of all our neuroses. If he is correct, then he is warning us that those few who have developed their creativity are set up for misunderstanding, envy, projection, and even violence. A culture that does not encourage creativity in all its members is a culture that is sending invitations out to people to maltreat those who are committed to creativity. A *New York Times* reporter once asked a very well-known feminist theologian why she was so caustic about my work. After some hesitation, the theologian replied that it was "academic envy." Envy is a form of projection. It is also a perverse form of flattery. It is a pity that academia rewards people for it. Envy, as I have indicated in my book, *Sins of the Spirit, Blessings of the Flesh*, kills community. It derives from the seventh chakra which, when healthy, actually builds community. But when the seventh chakra is misdirected, it kills what is beautiful in one another and what potentially could result in our working together to build together.

In a culture where Muzak reigns and the void is always being filled with noise of some kind, one must go out of one's way to find solitude and learn it. This is the role of meditation. Meditation becomes more important than ever for the survival of the imaginative mind. It is difficult to imagine creativity without it. The mystics talk about "gathering one's forces" and focusing. To gather one's forces is to leave the everyday noise behind one. One common way to meditate or gather one's forces is by honoring the breath. As Thich Nhat Hanh puts it: "Whenever your mind becomes scattered, use your breath as the means to take hold of your mind again." This practice results in mindfulness. A Hindu teacher says: "Without concentration, one can master nothing. Without concentration on Divinity, which shapes and controls the universe, one cannot unlock the Divinity within oneself or become a universal man." To meditate is to focus or concentrate. All artists need to focus and concentrate.

The irony exists that a culture or a person not at home with aloneness and solitude soon becomes swamped in loneliness. A cosmic loneliness takes over the soul when the soul can no longer feel the intimacy of communion with the many beloveds who bless us daily—from stars twinkling to grasses growing, from animals staring to flowers beaming. It takes a sense of inner silence to begin to appreciate the love and revelation and caring that are all around us in the other-than-human world. Loneliness feeds on a lack of aloneness, a dulled sensibility to solitude.

EXPECTING JOY: SPIRIT IS JOYFUL

Joy accompanies resurrection. I believe that one of the strongest sources of resistance to creativity is that we resist joy. We are afraid of joy. The absence of joy in our lives renders us guilty when we experience it ourselves and renders us resentful and envious when we see it in others. If we are artistes manqués, then we are also persons who are joie manquée. For joy comes with creativity, as the Hindu Scriptures teach us: "Where there is joy, there is creating. Know the nature of joy." The Christ in John's Gospel connects creativity and joy: "I commission you to go out and to bear fruit, fruit that will last. . . . I shall see you again, and your hearts will be full of joy, and that joy no one shall take from you" (John 15:16; 16:22). If, when we give birth, we are giving birth to the Cosmic Christ, then these promises of joy apply in a special way to our creative acts. The "second coming" (and the third and the fourth, ad infinitum) occurs when we give birth to the Christ, and with these births comes great joy.

For joy—lo and behold!—is integral to all creativity. Creativity brings joy. Just as love-making and bringing a child into the world brings joy, so, too, does writing a symphony, composing a song, singing a melody, dancing a dance, writing a book, giving a lecture, sharing one's poem, acting a part—all of these creative experiences bring joy with them. Painter David Paladin says when he looks upon his finished painting he feels a "sense of amazement," and the "joy of unbridled exploration, an unlimited source of inspiration," accompanies his painting.

Why is this? Since genuine creativity is characterized by an intensity of awareness and heightened consciousness, what the artist feels in doing art is felt very intensely. What is at the heart of the artist's feelings? Rollo May analyzes it this way: "What the artist or creative scientist feels is not anxiety or fear; it is joy. . . . The artist, at the moment of creating, does not experience gratification or satisfaction. . . . Rather, it is joy, joy defined as the emotion that goes with heightened consciousness, the mood that accompanies the experience of actualizing one's own potentialities."

I would go further than that. I would insist that what the artist is experiencing is far more than "actualizing one's own potentialities"—it is experiencing the Divine joy itself. Yielding to the creative act taps one in to the joy of creating, which is the Divine joy after all. Thomas Aquinas put it this way: "Sheer joy is God's and this demands companionship." In birthing, we are companions to the Birther of birthers— we are tapping in to the Divine joy at birthing, indeed at giving existence to creation itself. We are co-workers with God, co-birthers with God. Thus we are co-joyful with God the Creator. This is why all art work can be meditation itself: It is a discipline that opens us up to the joy of Divinity at work.

To be creative is to be, or to strive to be, intensely alive, intensely conscious. This is why joy accompanies the act of creativity. As Thomas Aquinas puts it: "Joy is the human's noblest act." Our noblest acts are joyful acts, but creativity brings joy—both to the artist and to the recipient of the art. Mothers have joy birthing (fathers, too), and hopefully the new child will experience joy as a gift from his or her parents. Joy is reciprocal. Joy is shareable without being lost or diminished. In fact, joy requires community to share it with. It reaches out to others. Like life does. Life yearns for life. Rollo May defines "creativity" in the following manner: "Creativity is the encounter of the intensively conscious human being with his or her world." An intensity accompanies creativity, and this intensity is directed to the world, that is to isness itself, to being, to what is, to creation, to life itself.

In a previous book, *Whee! We, Wee All the Way Home*, I use the term "ecstasy" to name the union of the Divine and us, a union that happens in nature, in friendship, in love-making, in suffering, in work, and in art. Rollo May also likes the term "ecstasy" to name what goes on in the creative act: "Ecstasy is the technical term for the process in which this union (of form and passion with order and vitality) occurs. . . . Ecstasy is the accurate term for the intensity of consciousness that occurs in the creative act. . . . It involves the total person." A union of God and us brings joy; this union can be called ecstasy. In ecstasy, the god of chaos and the god of order come together. May challenges the rationalism in our culture when he says that "it may well be that reason works best in the state of ecstasy. In ecstasy Dionysius, the god of chaos and madness, comes together with Apollo, the god of reason and order. We need this marriage to occur, we need to bring Dionysius and Apollo together."

The Divine encounter in acts of creativity involves more than our psyche and the Godhead. It involves the very act of ongoing creation in the universe. When we create, we are pouring being and gifts of being back into the universe itself. This pouring of being into the universe is a joyful act,

an ecstatic act. It takes us out of ourselves. Even if this ecstasy is for a brief moment only, we know and have tasted
and know that we know that we are part of a river of Spirit
that is far vaster and more beautiful and longer lasting than
ourselves. This ecstasy keeps us going. May names this experience as follows: "Insight and breakthrough happen and
only for that moment we participate in the myth of creation.
Order comes out of disorder, form out of chaos, as it did in
the creation of the universe. The sense of joy comes from
our participation, no matter how slight, in being as such."

These questions return: Are we up to all this joy? Are we
able to endure it? Will guilt or fear prevent us from taking it
on? Whence comes all this joy? For whom is it intended?
Are our souls large enough to welcome it? Can we recycle it
and make it energy for others and energy for other work?
Where in our training did anyone ever instruct us in how to
enjoy joy and do so without guilt? If we were able to answer
these questions, I think we might be able to redirect our
psyches and our civilization toward biophilia instead of
necrophilia. We would be able to redirect our civilization
toward creativity instead of its opposites—death, fear, guilt,
envy, loneliness, and joylessness.

EXPECTING LIFE: SPIRIT IS ALIVE!

Only those who have overcome a fear of death can truly live
and live fully. This is one more reason why the resurrection

story (or the reincarnation story or the regeneration story) is essential for a culture: Until we let go of our fear of death, we are not free to live fully. And living fully actually means to be creative. God, who is creative, lives fully and sends messengers who tell us they have come "so that you may have life and have it in abundance" (the Christ in John's Gospel). Wisdom brings life, Wisdom indeed is life: "This is wisdom: to love life" (Sirach 4:12). There is a passion that goes with living fully. Loving life, living life, creating life is passionate and erotic. Wisdom is eros, and eros is Wisdom.

With today's new creation story we are learning anew how fully committed the universe has been for its entire fourteen billion years of existence to creativity. Creativity is its thing; it is about constant birth and rebirth, life, death, and resurrection. Stars do it; galaxies do it; atoms do it; mountains do it; animals do it; birds do it; grasses do it. All of life, it turns out, is busy being creative. Why would *we* dare not to do it?

We cannot forget what life is. To the mystics, "God is Life." Thus, if we fear life, we fear God, and we will set up many, many false gods to assuage our fear of the real God. Fear will engender idols of many kinds, including religious idols, or fear of others different from ourselves, fear of diversity, fear of imagination, fear of empowerment of others, fear of joy, fear of life without guilt, fear of life without fear, fear of life in solitude, fear of death that is so overwhelming that it turns around to become an ultimate fear of life.

Rollo May poses a question that is a deserving one. He asks: "In our day of dedication to facts and hard-headed objectivity, we have disparaged imagination. . . . What if imagination and art are not frosting at all but the fountainhead of human experience?" Yes, the fountainhead of human experience. What if? What if creativity is, indeed, the fountainhead of human experience? What changes? Who changes? How do we change? What institutions change and how?

Cultural forces invade our world as well as our psyche. Some of these forces we have named as fear of death, fear of guilt, fear of loneliness, fear of joy, fear of life itself. It is little wonder that Rollo May calls the courage to create "the most important kind of courage of all." He elaborates: "Whereas moral courage is the fighting of wrongs, creative courage, in contrast, is the discovering of new forms, new symbols, new patterns on which a new society can be built. Every profession can and does require some creative courage. In our day, technology and engineering, diplomacy, business, and certainly teaching, all of these professions and scores of others are in the midst of radical change and require courageous persons to appreciate and direct this change."

So great is the resistance to creativity in our culture—we have found this resistance among religious fundamentalists as well as "liberal" academics, and we see it mirrored in our increasingly passive consumer culture—that we might compare our situation to the dire spiritual predicament that our Celtic ancestors called "soul-loss" or "soul fragmentation." One scholar has written: "Soul-loss may involve mental disorientation, emotional deadness or psychic depression; in severe cases, it may involve loss of consciousness."

In the Celtic understanding, dire occurrences come about because the soul is disrespectful to certain spirits, especially fairy spirits. Might we translate this diagnosis to suggest that in our culture the disrespect shown creativity is rendering us sick of soul and indeed without soul? The Celts felt that "jealousy was a strong and overriding cause of soul-displacement." In a similar vein, the projections of the artiste manqué onto the creative ones in a community can indeed carry on soul-loss in a community. With jealousy comes a compulsion to control. "Soul-theft occurs when an individual purposely attempts to intimidate or steal the vitality, goodness or virtue of another, or to bind the soul to their service. Soul-theft is most often attributed to the evil eye, when the vitality and energy of all living beings is sapped by an 'over-looker' who is jealous of its powers. Jealousy is one of the strongest motives for soul-theft—a manipulative readjustment of the life-force which is much feared and which is a major feature of Celtic protective invocations."

It is telling that soul-theft is attributed to the "evil eye," since the evil eye corresponds to the sixth chakra. It is a misuse of our creative powers, a using of them for evil purposes. (See my book *Sins of the Spirit* for sixth-chakra work and creativity.)

Sometimes grief causes soul-loss. There is plenty of grief in the human species today. And plenty of soul-loss.

For where creativity is lost, soul is lost. How did the Irish peoples bring soul back that had been lost, fragmented, or stolen? The method was to find the thread or track of the soul and coax it home. Healers, who were holy people, were employed and often brought with them their music, especially the healing harp. The help of deities and spirits was necessary as well. Sleep played an important role in healing. Song was invoked to sing the soul home. Saint Brighid offered a threefold protection since she is the Lady of Smithcraft, Healing, and Poetry "concerned with the weaving together of the mental, emotional and psychic strands which make life worthwhile. Celtic people have always invoked her to wrap her mantle of protection around them, for her mantle is nothing less than the web of life which defines the soul-shrine."

If these methods prove fruitful for us to retrieve our souls, i.e., our creativity, in our time, the irony lies in this: To do so will require artists—ritual artists, chanting artists, praying artists, saintly artists—to help bring this healing about. It seems that our cultural soul-loss may prove to be a benefit to all those committed to the creative path.

THE HOLY SPIRIT AS A WILD SPIRIT

Life is wild. Life is a wild ride, a ride between the highs and the lows, the mountains and the valleys, the via positiva and the via negativa. Nature is wild. We come from the wild—from the surging seas of the ocean, from the heat-blasting, hydrogen-exploding sun, from the supernovas bursting, from galaxies expanding, from the cooking fireball: We are made of wild stuff. Carbon, oxygen, sulphur, magnesium—we are very, very combustible. There is fire inside of us as well as water. There is revolution as well as peace. There is the familiar, and there is the shockingly new.

I have a friend who is an artist, and periodically he asks me: "Am I crazy?" This is an honest question. There are those who lead life more at the edge than the rest of us—Jesus, Gandhi, and King are among them. So do many other artists. The artist is so curious, so eager to stretch his or her soul, that sometimes boundaries are blurred and breakdown can occur. So many of the artists we have come to admire—Van Gogh, Mahler, and others—suffered severe mental hardship through their devotion to their art. Rollo May comments that genius and psychosis are very close to each other. If we are to welcome creativity in ourselves and one another, we must also welcome back a sense of the wild, which is, as Thomas Berry insists, a sense of the sacred. The wild is that which is bigger than us. So, too, is the sacred. Creativity has something of the wild about it—and something of the sacred.

There is a sense in which we ought to fear the sacred, but with what Aquinas calls a "chaste fear." We have a word for fear of the wild that is sacred. That word is "awe." (from which we also get the words "awful" and "awesome"). Awe is about chaste fear, healthy fear. Not a fear that freezes us or shrinks us into non-action or addiction or defensiveness or denial, but a fear that invites us to stretch and grow and trust. This fear results in courage, for it challenges us to explore, not to run away. And in the exploring come new learning and new growth. This fear grows our souls instead of shrinking them. It does not result in projections but in expansiveness. We remember vividly our whole life long the special moments of awe. We remember them as sacred moments.

Things go on in our psyches when we let creativity through that challenges our everyday control of things or that challenge our culture's definitions of what appropriate behavior might be. Part of standing up to fear of death, fear of guilt, fear of aloneness, fear of joy, and fear of life is standing up to take in the wild. Whatever the cost.

There are some wild things I cannot do. I cannot handle rattlesnakes or anacondas or live among the wolves as one friend of mine, a filmmaker, carver, and painter, does. But I do renew my creativity by walking near the sea as it rages and by walking near the waters when they are calm, by reading the mystics, who are wild poets of the wild soul, and by learning to laugh at self, soul, and others. Sometimes we spend so much effort trying to keep our wildness in check that it is humorous.

I can also resist the temptation to domesticate. When we domesticate self, God, or other beings, we are defanging them, emasculating them, removing the wild from them.

This is not a good spiritual practice. There must be some wildness left in our lives.

Foolishness and wisdom go together, after all, and folly is a certain response to wildness. To follow one's imagination is often an act of folly, a wild act deserving of Spirit's presence. For Spirit itself is wild, very, very wild. And we are sons and daughters of Spirit—and receptors for Spirit, and more than that: We are transmitters of Spirit. Spirit and we create together. We are, after all, co-creators. We can trust Spirit. We must trust Spirit. We must trust the wild again.

Meister Eckhart says that the Spirit can "madden us and drive us out of our senses." He is correct. There will be those who do not want to encounter a Spirit like that. But they are making a wrong choice. The Spirit fills *and* empties. It digs great caverns in our soul and sometimes—not always—it fills them up. The artist in us must yield to the Spirit in these matters. And in the yielding will be born the expansion of soul that courage requires and creativity demands. It is good that at least once in a while we associate with a Spirit capable of "maddening us and driving us out of our senses."

It is good that we yield to something more imaginative than the mere rational, the wholly objective. Getting lost is part of the spiritual journey. Jesus got lost in the temple at twelve, and we are all here to get lost, even to get intoxicated and drunk. Not on outside stimulants, you understand, but on existence itself, on creation itself. "They shall get drunk on the fullness of thy house," says the psalmist. And Aquinas comments "that is, the universe." We are here to get lost, get high, fall in love, go mad with the wonder of it all. In the madness there is a kind of union. A union with all the creators and co-creators who are bringing something truly new into the universe, the true disturbers of the peace. Here we learn anew the wisdom in the phrase "the fierce power of imagination is a gift from God." For God gives to some of her children a special gift, which we might call the courage to be mad, to be outside the mainstream, to live and dance on the edge of life where psyche and cosmos meet, where Spirit flows into the human, where only the angels have the sure-footedness to tred lightly. Rumi offers the following advice:

We must become ignorant
Of all we've been taught,
And be, instead, bewildered.

Run from what's profitable and comfortable
If you drink those liqueurs, you'll spill
The spring water of your real life.

Forget safety.
Live where you fear to live.
Destroy your reputation.
Be notorious.

I have tried prudent planning
Long enough, from now
On, I'll live mad.

Angels and spirits often accompany the journey of creativity. As I indicated in a previous book, angels learn exclusively by intuition, and so they are partial to those among us who have learned to trust their intuition and also learn that way. I am speaking of the artist in us and among us. Artists invariably meet angels on the highway of intuition. Angels assist us in our making of connections. M. C. Richards captured this relationship in a poem when she writes:

> We gather into an ear, a glance, an embrace
> to receive our angels. Around us they hover,
> plaiting their feathers, gazing into the crystal
> of the inner eye, holding the neck of a wild swan. . . .
> Our worlds are one, they say. Look! They are all about us! . . .
> weaving and dancing, afire with high heat, pale and
> pearl-like, silvery, and carved like hard wood. What
> are they singing? "In art is a communion of worlds!"

There are those in our culture who think one is mad to speak of angels. But these are people living a one-dimensional, rational, existence. We miss a lot if we ignore the realm of the angels. M. C. Richards continues:

> A flutter of feathers, a song, a
> stir of air—"Keep the faith,"
> they sing: "human dreams are angel food,
> human deeds are angel drink.
> When you gather together like this,

imagination deepens across the heavens,
and we see your souls trafficking between the worlds.
Through the crossing point pours a living fountain;
your art will guide you to its waters.
Farewell. We are with you always. Feel
in your inner eye our iris crystal
and under your feet the web of the swan."

I know many people who have had direct or indirect experience of angels. Indeed, every culture in the world—except the modern world of the past few centuries—acknowledges the presence and the experience of spirits and angels. We ignore them to our peril. Even scientists such as Rupert Sheldrake and Alfred Russel Wallace, a companion to Charles Darwin, grant the presence of angels in the unfolding of the work of evolution.

To ignore the angels is to ignore some of the most benign experiences of wildness at our disposal. For angels are wild. They are big. They are smart. They are very speedy, traveling as they do at the speed of light. They are intelligent. They carry "ideas from prophet to prophet," according to Aquinas. This could be amended to say: "They carry ideas from artist to artist." And they are loving—indeed, Aquinas says that angels "cannot help but love." Thomas Aquinas teaches that angels convey Divine enlightenment and revelation to humans, that "the Spirit works grace in people by means of the angels," that prophecy is carried out by angels, and that "angels are always announcers of Divine silence." This implies that when we encounter silence we are encountering angels. Angels travel great distances to witness our creativity and to encourage it.

Why would we ever willingly cut out such powerful beings from our lives? Why not invoke them for our creative journeys? Maybe they can assist us when our culture's institutions are most failing us. If they are as integral to creation and to music as cultures worldwide teach us, then it is hard to imagine living a cosmology that excludes them. Let us link up with these wild spirits, then, and ask them to keep our spirits wild and free as well. And our work. That it may deserve to be called the work of the Spirit. After all, the angels were said to be active in the rolling away of the boulder from the tomb of Jesus.

Among the spirits we might profit from calling upon is the spirit that Dr. Clarissa Pinkola Estés names the "Wild Woman." She is, says Estés, "patroness to all painters, writers, sculptors, dancers, thinkers, prayermakers, seekers, finders— for they are all busy with the work of invention, and that is the Wild Woman's main occupation. As in all art, she resides in the guts, not in the head. . . . She is the one who thunders after injustice." The Wild Woman carries us beyond mere coping or mere surviving to *thriving*. And thriving means, among other things, creating. Sometimes we become a "lone wolf" in the process of thriving, we find ourselves "standing on the edge, [which] means one is practically guaranteed to make an original contribution, a useful and stunning contribution to her culture." So essential is our courage at this point that we can say: "If you have ever been called defiant, incorrigible, forward, cunning, insurgent, unruly rebellious, you're on the right track. Wild Woman is close by. If you have never been called these things, there is yet time. Practice your Wild Woman." And men, practice your Wild Man.

Seeing Easter as an overcoming of the fear of death and the obstacles to creativity, putting grace before guilt, embracing solitude, expecting joy as well as life, and welcoming Spirit as a *wild* Spirit—all these practices allow us to roll away the obstacles to creativity just as the angels rolled away the boulders from the entombed Christ.

{seven}

tapping into the creative spirit: finding, honoring, and practicing creativity

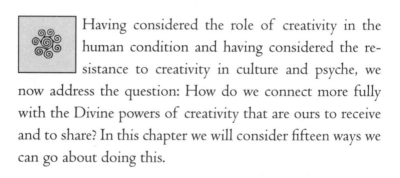 Having considered the role of creativity in the human condition and having considered the resistance to creativity in culture and psyche, we now address the question: How do we connect more fully with the Divine powers of creativity that are ours to receive and to share? In this chapter we will consider fifteen ways we can go about doing this.

1. Learn to Praise

As we pointed out in chapter 3, the *via positiva*, that is to say, the experience of falling in love, is a requisite for creativity. Falling in love opens the soul up, it expands the heart, it triggers a way of being in us that allows our soul to soar like an eagle and ride the waves like an adroit surfer. Falling in love is far too necessary an experience to be limited only to finding a two-legged mate. We can and need to fall in love daily with nature's ongoing beauty, which is all around us. Dr. Clarissa Estés sees creativity as deriving from the power of being in love: "It is the love of something, having so much love for something—whether a person, a word, an image, an idea, the land, or humanity—that all that can be done with the overflow is to create. It is not a matter of wanting to, not a singular act of will; one solely must."

Praise is the word we speak when we are in love. Without praise, there is no real art; there is only ego-art. With praise, the human is doing what we were birthed by the universe to do: to tell the truth of the wonders and the goodness of what is. Learning to praise is the opposite of taking for granted. It is *taking notice*. Following is a litany of praise of some of the beings that we share this planet with and who are themselves busy being creative all day long. Much of the commentary is drawn from the elegant spiritual tradition of Taoism, which has honored the exquisite spirituality intrinsic to all nature for centuries.

1. Let Us Learn to Praise the Earth

Earth is called "mother" in many human cultures for a reason. "All growth comes from the earth," say the Taoists. The ancients put the question: "What is bountiful?" And the answer was "not the treasury of the emperor, but the generosity of the earth. The golden hills provided home, country, belonging. The rich, black, fertile-smelling soil gave grain, vegetables, and fruit. The blue-shadowed mountains gave shelter from wind and storm. And the seemingly end-less plains and deserts provided ample room for exploration and adventure." There is so much to praise in the earth—its seasons, its generativity, its diversity, its oceans and rocks, its grasses and critters, its uniqueness in developing just the right balance of discipline and order, which results in such abundant variety growing here.

Minerals and jewels, water and flowers, trees and plants—what an endless litany of beings useful and beautiful the earth births and nurtures day and night. How could we ever take the earth for granted? How could we ever cease praising the earth? How could we not notice or not care?

The Taoists say: "If you want to follow Tao, first under-stand the perfection of heaven and earth." Learning to study the Tao may be as simple and as at hand as bending down and picking up a handful of earth.

2. Let Us Learn to Praise the Sky

The masters of Taoism, when asked how to find the Tao, pointed one hand to the sky and the other hand to the earth. This profound gesture "places human beings between heaven and earth, but also after heaven and earth in impor-tance. . . . It also serves as a reminder that people are a part of all things under heaven."

The modern era effectively desacralized, and in the process even desecrated, the sky for us. We were told that the universe was a machine, which translated means that the sky is dead and full of cold, dead parts like pieces of a machine. No life there, nothing to wonder at, no growth, no mysteries to commune with, no beings to connect to. Fortunately, today's science is discarding the "dead sky" theory and returning to a place of primal fascination with the sky. "Father Sky," once killed by modern science and philosophy, is coming alive again. This is especially good news, because now men, who in so many cultures are taught about "Mother Earth, Father Sky," can find their souls again and rediscover how robust and vast, how wild and full of life, fatherhood can and ought to be. Fatherhood ought to be an imitation of the heavens themselves.

Of course the very word "heaven" has also lost its meaning during the modern era. If it is true that "hell" means concealment, then "heaven" must mean revelation. The skies, the heavens, are full of revelation. The wonders; the birth, death, and resurrection of galaxies and stars and planets; the amazing black holes that suck in beings all around them—all this is a revelation, an unveiling, of the great mysteries of nature's profound creativity. The sky is busy creating: It is our origin, even more ancient than the earth. From its matrix the atoms were born, the galaxies, supernovas, stars, and planets, including our own earth, came to be, and these form the very stuff of our existence.

The Pascal mystery of life, death, and resurrection applies to the sky. We are all connected. Our ancestors, the very communion of saints, includes the sky beings that are our ancient parents and who are still begetting and birthing after all these billions of years.

The word used for "sky" in Chinese Taoism, *tian,* means "sky," "heaven," and "nature." Tao was to be discerned in heaven, nature, and the sky. The sky is "endless, vast, ever present yet ever changing. . . . The wind blows through its blue expanse. The clouds gather and disappear in its vastness. Without its air we could not breathe. Without the sun, we could not live." The sky reminds us of our own expansiveness and greatness. Our spirit cannot be content "unless it has a greatness as vast as the sky's in which to roam." The sky contains the history of our origins. We are learning this from the Hubble telescope and other telescopes, from probings of Mars and the moon and more. The sky is like an archaeological library of the cosmos and its history. By exploring it, we explore our own histories; by visiting it, we learn our place and time in the universe. We even learn some wisdom and some humility, for as Taoism teaches: "Heaven is always greater than humanity." It is easy to learn to praise the sky.

3. Let Us Learn to Praise the Water

"Water is life," we are told by Taoist teachings. Science tells us the same thing. No water = no life. Water = life or possible life. Thus we are probing Mars for evidence of water even if only in the distant past. Might life have existed or even still exist on Mars? Or on Jupiter's moons where we have found ice, is there also water beneath the ice and perhaps life in those waters?

In ancient China, the Tao was compared to water, because water is flowing, powerful, profound, unafraid, balanced, nourishing, still, and pure. "One who would follow Tao need only emulate water in every way," we are told. Water is unafraid, because "from any height, it will plunge fearlessly down. It will fall and not be injured." Indeed, as we all know, a waterfall presents one of life's most beautiful and powerful experiences.

We all need water to live. Water is essential. We share our need for water with all the plants, trees, animals, birds, fishes. Water bespeaks the unconscious because of its depths and the mysteries it houses in those depths. The Age of Aquarius, in which we now find ourselves, is an age supposedly of the "water bearer," an age when our species will be looking for depth and will travel deeper. An age of spirituality, therefore, of bringing mystery up and the unconscious alive. An age of wetness and fertility, we hope.

Water is also feminine. Water flows. The yin power of water stills us and calms us, for water can be very calming and can be "completely still, and in its stillness, mirror heaven perfectly." Of course, water can also be unbearably wild and ferocious and destructive as in a flood or in a "perfect storm" at sea. Water is extremist—it touches both the contemplative and the wildly active side of nature and so teaches us about human nature itself which, like water, is destined for both stillness and wildness, calm and storm.

Water is soft, "yet when its force accumulates, it can level mountains." Water gathers together other waters, rivulets become rivers, rivers become oceans. In this way, too, we are to gather up our various forces, and "when all the parts of our life join with each other, the force of our personality becomes great." How is this possible? Water teaches the way: the way is that of humility. For water always seeks the lower ground. It is there, by filling caverns and deep places, that water gathers its strength. We can do the same.

A recent study by Masaru Emoto, a doctor of alternative medicine in Japan, furnishes pictures of frozen water crystals that are truly remarkable. His book, *Messages from Water*, demonstrates that water crystals respond differently to music by Bach and Mozart than to hard rock. (Bach and Mozart form beautiful crystals of various formations; hard rock does not.) If you write "I love you" or "Thank you" on a glass of water, the crystals are harmonious and beautiful; if you say "I despise you," the crystals are clouded and ugly. This study is all the more amazing when we consider that 70 percent of our bodies is water, and 70 percent of the earth is water. "Water is a mirror reflecting our mind," Dr. Emoto concludes. When we pray and project good thoughts into water, it responds accordingly. His five-year experiment of photographing water amazed the experimenters. "We did not expect . . . that the crystals would show such dramatic and clear changes. We have become aware that water stores and transmits information."

4. Let Us Learn to Praise Our Ability to See What Is

The schools one attended to learn Taoism were not indoors. The books for learning Taoism were not printed books.

Learning Taoism occurred when the young went walking with the older ones. Students who wanted to see Tao were shown animals and trees, they were led through tiger-filled mountains and flower-covered valleys, they forded icy rivers and crossed sun-scorched deserts. In this way, "the ancients showed the way of the world in its limitless variety. What was so important about this method is that the ancients trusted their students to see. They trusted their students' perceptions." They also trusted nature's capacity as a teacher. They trusted the human mind's curiosity and its capacity to see what is. It was taken for granted that understanding happens because a kind of built-in relationship exists between the human and the rest of nature. Expose an inquiring mind to nature and it will learn. Nature is teacher; human is student.

Instead of elaborate rituals or fancy words, Taoism was taught through observation. "They simply let their students live and travel with them, and they knew that the students would see Tao in the wind and mountains, trees and rivers, animals and people. The real Tao wasn't inaccessible. The real Tao was the everyday Tao." And the everyday Tao was accessed through seeing and observing what is. It is available to everybody. It is utterly democratic. "The idea that each of us can be directly spiritual is radical. . . . If we want to see Tao, we need only open our eyes and trust what we see." Let us learn to praise our powers of observation and understanding.

5. Let Us Learn to Praise the Rocks

Rocks are the most ancient peoples on earth. They are our elders. The Lakota people know this well; when they pray, they pray with heated rocks in sweat lodges. The rocks are the old people; they are the elders that bring toxins out of us and holy prayers as well. One of the most revered names for the Great Spirit among the Lakota people is Tagashala, which means "Grandfather of the Rock People." How much the rocks have to teach us! How stalwart and enduring they are. Yet how beautiful and diverse and full of stories and years and years of being worked on by water, sun, rain, earth, and people. They are patient; they are strong; they are good teachers.

Taoists, too, honor the rocks. "Those of us who aspire to meditation need only become like a rock." We can choose the right time to imitate water and the right time to imitate rock. "Know when to be a rock. A rock is stable. It cannot be forced into being something it is not. It knows how to meditate. A rock can be a bulwark against the rain of misfortune."

6. Let Us Learn to Praise the Trees

The tree people and their immediate ancestors were the first living creatures to defy gravity, to walk upright, to leave the sea that served as a floating home and to dare to grow themselves on land. Now their sap (which would develop into our blood), instead of circulating through the organism as it floated in the sea, dared to travel up and down. We would not be here had the trees failed in their experiment. We owe so much to trees.

Fred Hageneder has written a powerful book, *The Spirit of Trees*, which reminds us all of what we owe trees. He writes: "Trees are the most successful life forms on Earth. . . . Societies of trees are fundamental to weather and climate, for a beneficial water cycle; for the development of minerals; for balancing the electrical charges between the ionosphere and the Earth's surface; and for the maintenance of the Earth's magnetic field as a whole. In addition, their intelligent and adaptable design, and their ability to co-operate, have made trees the dominant life form on Earth since they first appeared more than three hundred million years ago."

So sacred are trees that all cultures consecrated woodlands for sacred ceremonies. These sacred groves were visited for purposes of prayer, meditation, or thanksgiving. Fire that drove human development was possible only because of the wood retrieved from trees. Celts, Druids, Romans, Greeks, Egyptians, Indians of India, and the Israelites had a special attraction to the tree. The menorah represents the Tree of Life and is itself the Tree of Light with its seven branches. Buddha was not only awakened under a tree but for many centuries he was depicted *as a tree*. "The Bodhi tree—and not Buddha—was called *the Great Awakener.*"

Taoism teaches us: "A tree uses what comes its way to nurture itself." It sinks roots into the earth for nourishment, it accepts rain by shedding water from its leaves to the ground and to its roots. It stands and stands all day and all night with huge limbs outstretched—it is strong, and it teaches us strength. Trees know how to absorb our pain and help us to recycle our grief. I often walk among the redwood trees that absorb pain profoundly. "Absorb, absorb, absorb. That is the secret of the tree," say the Taoists. It is also a secret to our existence. "Accept what life sends you. Accept how Tao flows through you, just as the tree absorbs and grows, and you will never be without Tao." Let us praise the trees.

7. *Let Us Learn to Praise the Animals*
Taoists, being committed to observation of nature as a spiritual exercise, learned much from observing the animals. Two animals that were particularly revelatory to the ancients were the crane and the tiger.

The crane has a proud profile. Though it has very thin legs, it can stand for hours on just one leg—strength is learned from the crane. The crane is very observant in its hunt for fish. "Above all, everything we need to know about vigilance can be learned from the crane. . . . The crane combines vigilance and movement. Those are exactly the qualities we need to go through life and to follow Tao." Vigilance is not passive, and it is not just waiting. It includes acting but acting at the right time. Vigilance "is a matter of the correct timing."

The tiger represents energy and force. "Once we awaken to Tao, the force of our own spirit will be as strong as a tiger's." There is a vitality in the tiger that is pure energy. This can be ours as well. Tales exist among the Chinese about tigresses who rescued children, offered them their own milk, and raised them in the wild. A true Taoist combines the ferocity of the tiger with the gentleness of nurturing.

There exist noble tigers and killing tigers. The former use their skills to instruct others, "spread contentment, and cultivate enlightenment." The latter use their skills "to enslave others, topple kingdoms, and seek immortality. They were like killing tigers." Evil people imitate killing tigers. We need to choose what we will do with our tiger energy, what we will use it for.

There is so much to praise. We have only begun a simple list of the gifts of nature around us that deserve praise. We have talked of earth and sky, of rocks and trees, of water and understanding, of animals such as the crane and the tiger. We could also talk of fireball and hydrogen atoms, of galaxies and supernovas, of carbon and oxygen and sulfur, of sun and moon, of stars and planets—the list is unending. We could talk of music and musicians, paintings and painters, pots and potters, poems and poets, bridges, cities and engineers, rituals and ritual-makers—is there any end to the Litany of Praise that our species is capable of? Why hold back? Creativity begins with praise.

Praise is all-powerful. Praise moves the soul and cleanses the soul. It even shifts the soul and rescues it from those powers of cynicism and thanatos that are capable of stealing our souls from us. That is why praise is a path to healing and to waking up, a path to getting over our wounds and deep hurts and abuses and becoming fully present again to that which is praiseworthy, i.e., to life and its many gifts: to creation and its diverse beauties, wonders, and relationships. That is why Hildegard of Bingen, among others, urges us to "be not lax in celebration. Be not lazy in the festive service of God. Be ablaze with enthusiasm. Let us be an alive, burning offering before the altar of God!" Praise is celebration, and celebration is praise.

Praise is the utterance of appreciation. It also increases our appreciation, for when we praise with others we absorb their gratitude at the same time that we utter our own. In listening to what Taoists have appreciated in earth, sky, water, understanding, rocks, trees, and animals, we have increased our own sense of appreciation. Praise begets praise. Appreciation begets appreciation. That is good. That is necessary. That is salvific. That lights our fires of creativity.

2. Open Oneself to Joy

Opening ourselves to joy is not that different from learning to praise. Praise is the noise that joy makes, after all. But it deserves saying, since joy opens our hearts to the expansion that creativity is all about. We have to work at finding joy since there is so much in our culture that entices us (or tries to entice us) away from joy to pseudo-joys and pseudo-highs. True joy is an inside thing. True joy does not come from the outside. True joy is, therefore, nonaddictive. Joy is what happens when we join the joyful powers of the universe again. To do this we must prepare ourselves, we must be willing to let go and let joy happen. We must let go of dictating what our joy will be (for example, "when I get this pay raise" or "find this boyfriend" or "buy this car"). Desire has a place in our lives, but joy is deeper than desire. It will not be dictated to. It will not be bought and paid for.

To know joy, we must know the heart. We must live where the heart lives. There is no other path to real joy. We need to be expectant of authentic joy; we might even say we need to believe in joy, to believe it is possible. And to disbelieve, to cut our beliefs in cynicism off at the root. If there is joy in the heart of all creatures, then we, too, are on that path and have ample opportunity and are invited to join the universe that is eminently joyful.

Joy has something to do with finding our right relationships to what is. That is why creativity brings such joy. Creativity requires our right relationship to the powers of birthing that permeate the universe and want to flow through us as well. When Thomas Aquinas says that "joy is the human's noblest act," he is urging us to put joy forward as a priority in our work and in all our relations. He is also urging us to imitate the Creator, since he believes that "God is supremely joyful and therefore supremely conscious." To become joyful is to become conscious—aware, awake, alert, caring. Passion and joy go together.

All spiritual traditions instruct us to expect joy. Buddha said: "Be a joy unto yourself." The Upanishads of ancient Hinduism say: "Joy comes from God.... From joy all beings have come and unto joy they all return." Rabbi Abraham

Joshua Heschel teaches that "joy is a way to God" and that "all joy comes from God," for "to sense the living God is to sense infinite goodness, infinite wisdom, infinite beauty. Such a sensation is a sensation of joy." And Julian of Norwich teaches us that "the fullness of joy is to behold God in everything."

8. Enter the Dark

When darkness comes in the form of pain or disappointment, betrayal or discouragement, depression or failure, our natural tendency is to run. The Sufi mystic Hafiz put it well in the following poem:

> Love wants to reach out and manhandle us,
> > Break all our teacup talk of God. . . .
> The Beloved sometimes wants
> > To do us a great favor:
> > Hold us upside down
> And shake all the nonsense out.
> > But when we hear
> He is in such a "playful drunken mood"
> > Most everyone I know
> Quickly packs their bags and hightails it
> > Out of town.

This "flight" response is to be expected. It is not to be followed, however. So much of our culture is in flight from the darkness. How much of our drug addiction, our alcohol addiction, our shopping, sexual, work, television, religious, and relationship addictions are efforts at fleeing the suffering of life?

Buddha observed, and rightly so, that life entails suffering. All beings suffer. Even hydrogen atoms suffered as they were cooked and birthed in the original fireball. Many did not make it to the next step of their evolution. Those who did must have been mightily thankful, however. The continents that were wrenched apart some two hundred and fifty million years ago might have suffered, too, to lose their motherland and to have to drift off and be separate for what seems like forever. Stars live, but they also die. All beings suffer as they participate in the great drama called creation.

Why should humans be any different? Why should we be spared what all other beings have undergone? Of course we are not spared. Perhaps our suffering seems greatest of all because we live for so brief a period and because our highly developed consciousness is so vulnerable and sensitive to pain and can even anticipate it so deeply that we can die of anxiety and the future of pain that has not yet happened. We can also so mull over the past that we can die of the pain from the past as well.

We are urged by Buddha and other spiritual teachers to take the middle road when it comes to pain. Not to deny it and not to stir it up, but to be with the pain, to let pain be pain and ask what it has to teach us. Pain is a teacher. The darkness is a teacher. The shadow is a teacher. Those who awaken our shadows are teachers. Even evil is a teacher.

Jesus taught people to "enter the dark." He went off to

Jerusalem, knowing that a call for his blood was in the air. He set off anyway. It's not that he didn't fear death, not that he didn't care to cling to life. It is just that he loved the quality of life he was teaching more than he feared death. His light overcame the darkness, even the darkness of fear of death. Martin Luther King, Jr., also knew about death threats and the darkness of hatred and racism in men's hearts. Yet he kept going anyway. And he confessed that he had learned that one had to love something more than the fear of death if one were to live fully. He lived fully. His death was an integration into his life and all he stood for in his life. It was tragic, it was awful, it was premature. But it was also redemptive for the rest of us. He showed us the way—by his teachings, by his life, *and* by his death. He showed us courage and how we can all enter the dark and not be lost there but actually be saved there.

Creativity requires the darkness as well as the light, suffering as well as joy. Could flowers grow if they were in the sun twenty-four hours per day? Even the sky rests in darkness; our psyches sleep in darkness nightly; all creativity takes a break in the dark. The artist in us needs to learn and relearn to welcome the dark and to be at home there. Repose is good. It is necessary. It refreshes and awakens our imaginations for new insights, new revelations, new visitors. Angels often come at night when our defenses are down to lead us to our creative work the next morning. As the Prometheus story tells us, the liver (the cleansing organ) does renew itself in the dark, during the night. And creativity goes on no matter how many vultures are eating away at us during the daytime hours.

The creative person learns to be at home in the dark. Poet Pablo Neruda puts it this way: "All paths lead to the same goal: to convey to others what we are. And we must pass through solitude and difficulty, isolation and silence, in order to reach forth to the enhanced place where we can dance our clumsy dance and sing our sorrowful song—but in this dance or in this song there are fulfilled the most ancient rites of our conscience in the awareness of being human and of being in common destiny." Notice that Neruda is encouraging us to go through both the via positiva and the via negativa in a strong way, because by learning to tell our deep story we tap into the "ancient rites" of our collective conscience as a species. Indeed, this is powerful motivation to come to our place of creativity.

Actress Holly Hunter was once interviewed about a part she played in a play by Irish playwright Marina Carr. Her character was very dark in spirit. Says Hunter: "That's the pact you make. If you want to create and you want to be a creator in any way, creativity is about darkness. Because it's in all of us; it's part of being alive. And I think there's a need, culturally, to express that. It's illegal to express it in many ways in our society, so the legal way to express it, without hurting people, is in the arts. And then you can take any trip you want."

Dancer Martha Graham tasted deeply of darkness and suffered some severe depressions in her lifetime. Yet it has been said that her "crises infused, rather than crippled, her art." Graham sacrificed much for her love of dance and her vocation to dance. For this revolution to occur, Graham points out, "there was a revolt against the ornamented forms of impressionistic dancing. There came a period of great austerity." Such austerity is a kind of darkness as well, a voluntary accepting of darkness. Her friend Agnes de Mille put it this way: "Martha felt that she must cut from her life all deep emotional involvements, all attachments, all comforts, even moments of leisure, and beyond that, love involving family and children. She gave everything to her work, withheld nothing, kept nothing apart. She was obsessed."

Graham saw the discipline it takes to become a dancer as part of the price one paid for giving back a gift. "The body must be tempered by hard, definite technique—the science of dance movement—and the mind enriched by experience," she observed. She felt that it took ten years of hard work to become a dancer. "It took years to become spontaneous and simple. Nijinsky took thousands of leaps before the memorable one," she remarked. In creating new forms for modern dance, Graham and her troop were stepping on the toes of others. "We risked everything; every one of us had thrown overboard all of our tradition," comments De Mille. The gifts we have received come with a price, as psychologist Howard Gardner observes. Are we willing to pay a price to return that gift to the community, to the Gift-giver? Are we up to the generosity and sacrifice that giving often requires?

Navajo painter David Paladin was put in a Nazis concentration camp at the age of fifteen. He suffered such torture that when he was liberated two and a half years later, he weighed sixty-two pounds and was a paraplegic. He was in a coma for two years, but his elders taught him that all that pain was an initiation into becoming a shaman. He says: "Shamans know that those wounds are not theirs but the world's. Those pains are not theirs but Mother Earth's. You can gift the world as shaman because you're a wounded warrior. A wounded healer and a wounded warrior are one." Instead of returning pain for pain, the warrior-shaman raises above his own dead body and says, "I have died, too. Now let's dance. We're free. The spirit is ours because we have died. Now we are resurrected from the ashes."

9. Study and Learn

Toxic attitudes of anti-intellectualism and super-rationalism have contributed to our being out of touch with the ancient teaching that study and learning are a prayer. Study is a mode of entrance to the Creative Spirit. In the Jewish tradition, to study Torah is a prayerful act. Thomas Aquinas, writing from the Dominican tradition in the early thirteenth century, concurs. Learning and teaching are more noble for arousing devotion, he maintains, than even chanting or singing.

Just because artists do right-brain work and exercise their intuitions in depth does not mean that left-brain work is not important. Indeed, without the work of study and learning the artist may lack both the tools of one's craft *and* the awareness of what to say, what topics to address, what stories to tell that speak to us of the pain of our species at a particular time and in a particular culture. Aquinas understood art to be an "intellectual virtue" along with science, prudence, wisdom, and understanding. Without study, one's work can fall into mere ego-tripping or ego-protection or self-indulgence. Study opens up a bigger world to us than our personal emotions and personal story alone. In fact, study connects our personal emotions and personal story to the bigger story of others. It grows the soul by growing the mind, and it grows the heart in the same process. The heart can only love what it is exposed to, what it knows. It stands to reason, then, that to expand knowledge is to expand the possibilities for the heart's falling in love as well.

It is my deepest conviction, based on my own personal experience as well as observation, that learning is one of the most spiritual, ecstatic, mystical, and prayerful experiences available to us all. I write books in order to learn. That is what makes it so fun—even when much drudgery is involved. Learning (unlike education, alas!) is non-elitist—we can all do it. It is available to everyone with senses and with a mind still intact. Our minds were made for learning just as our stomachs were made for eating, and, like eating, our learning ought to be delicious and healthy. Quality food for the mind is just as important as healthy food for the body. Society and parents alike ought to be making it very clear *by example* to our young ones how valuable and indispensable and delicious and fun the experience of learning can be. By example, adults who visit museums, play musical instruments, read, listen to music, hike, camp, and take care of their bodies are telling the young that the mind is happiest when it is learning.

All day long we can be learning. We learn from every being and every event we encounter in a day. We are never too old to learn and never too young to learn—which is one reason why the old and the young should mix on a regular basis. Diversity of all kinds is helpful to set an environment for curiosity, questioning, and therefore for learning. That is one reason why, when we retire at night, four good questions to put to ourselves are the following: What have I learned today? Who has learned something from me? Does what we are learning contribute to biophilia (love of life) more than to necrophilia (love of death)? Have I been busy spreading the seeds of biophilia today? As we saw above, Thich Nhat Hanh believes that we are born with seeds of violence and seeds of peace within each of us, but the latter have to be watered and nurtured to come to fruition. Nurturing corresponds to spreading seeds of biophilia, seeds of love of life, and passion for existence.

There are clearly many things we can be learning about daily. Our culture offers us the gossip of movie stars and politicians' lives, for example. The media loves to get us to talk about itself and take it as seriously as they do. What items are primal? What topics are the most useful at this time? What are the most important truths that we should be making an effort to learn about today?

I believe that we ought to be learning the new creation story from science and cosmology, because with a common cosmology our species can get moving again. Creatures lead us to the Divine. Aquinas says that "by dwelling on creatures the mind is inflamed to love the Divine goodness" and that we "love and know God in the mirror of God's creatures." If this is so, then we ought to be applying our learning to understanding the story of how creatures have arrived through the billions of years of the unfolding of the cosmos.

To apply ourselves to the study of creatures is to apply ourselves to Divine Wisdom itself. "Divine wisdom first appears in the creation of things," Aquinas observes. Creation becomes our doorway to the Divine Wisdom. Why take it for granted? Why ignore it? Why not conjure up our curiosity about our origins and with it begin to "inflame" the mind again to love the Divine goodness or blessing inherent in all creation?

I also believe that we ought to be learning spiritual wisdom traditions from around the world. This study of "deep ecumenism" gives us insight and a common language to look deeper into our own hearts and our own spiritual response to what is. Writing my recent book on deep ecumenism, *One River, Many Wells*, filled me with appreciation for living in this unique period of human history when we *can* access so many rich traditions and be challenged to explore our own traditions more deeply. No government or transnational corporation or institutional religion in itself holds the power for deep change and transformation that Wisdom Traditions hold.

The transformational effort on our part today must begin from within. It must begin with Spirit and spirituality. Therefore, we ought to be studying the healthy mystics, past and present, who present us with challenges and in-depth practices and who model by their words and their actions what it means to be a healthy and adult human being dedicated to bringing Spirit into the world.

Aquinas says that the contemplative life requires that we learn well-known truths but also that "one learns unknown things. The second is learned not only through Scriptures and creatures, but also interiorly." Thus the mystics teach us to trust our interior learning, our looking into our own hearts and souls, just as we look into creatures and into holy sacred texts. Meditation *is* a form of learning.

Part of searching our own hearts is looking for the amazement that is there. Rabbi Heschel says we are all capable of "radical amazement." When we study in order to be amazed, we are awakening Spirit in ourselves. As Aquinas put it, our desire to know is part of wonder itself: "From wonder a person proceeds to inquire. And this inquiry does not cease until she arrives at a knowledge of the essence of the cause." This is why Aquinas sees amazement as the "beginning of philosophical research." This explains to me why so many scientists I have queried over the years about the source of their vocation invariably refer to a moment of wonder or amazement as a young child. Imagine this! Wonder is so powerful, even when we are young, that it can set you on your life's course forever. How dare we underestimate the power of wonder! How dare we excise wonder from our schools, from our media which are teachers, from our homes or places of worship. It is time we reintroduced wonder into one another's lives.

To study our own hearts (with the help of other thinkers and tracers to the heart) is to rediscover *longing*. Longing needs to be addressed, needs to be listened to. What is it we really long for? Did we shelve this longing, give up on it, reject it, or tell ourselves other things were more important? There is sadness in longing, the sense of absence of what we long for. Longing also brings up fervor, an intense desire to be with the object of our longing. There is a place for longing, a place for both languor and fervor. The most dangerous decision is to reject longing, languor, and fervor altogether. That way lies death of Spirit. It is a way without creativity, a way without passion.

10. Honor the Child Inside and Play a Lot

Children, when they are allowed to be children, connect to their fantasies and connect to the powers of the universe, including communing in amazing ways with animals and other forces. Dr. Clarissa Estés observes the intimate connection between the child in us and the wild in us when she says: "Children *are* the wildish nature, and without being told. . . ."

Children are still capable of living in a world of wonder. To reconnect to wonder is to awaken the child inside, and to do that is to tap into all kinds of Creative Spirits and muses. In the tradition of Taoism, the symbol for "play" combines two symbols: one standing for "jade" and one for "origin" or "source." It is said, therefore, that "playing is as precious as jade and helps us find our way back to the beginning— the source." Play is a kind of meditation, for it takes us back to the Source of all things, including joy and beauty. We ought to follow this path regularly, and the more self-occupied and self-conscious and conceited a culture is (the more adultist, therefore), the more it needs to revivify itself through play.

Taoist Deng Ming-Dao says: "Those who follow Tao believe in fun and play. Through play, the letting go of our restrictions, the lighthearted association of disparate and 'irrational' elements, the turning over of established order, we open the way to our own creativity." We can and ought to recall the accomplishments of those who become creative while tinkering, taking a bath, eating breakfast, taking a walk, sipping tea, or just doing nothing. "A smart person takes play seriously, for in the act of playing is the possibility of going beyond established borders. And Tao, while it is everywhere, is most likely to be found outside of borders. If you want to be with Tao, it is better to put aside all that is 'important' and 'significant' and just play. Be natural. You'll arrive at Tao a lot sooner than if you make a 'special effort.'" Play is natural. We cannot be natural without playing.

It has been said that the artist "regresses" to a childhood capacity for play. This process, as Howard Gardner sees it, "involves a continual interplay between creation and criticism, manifested in the painter's alternation of working on the canvas and stepping back to observe the effect." Children are so often original because they are spontaneous. "The play impulse becomes the art impulse (supposing it strong enough to survive the play years) when it is illumined by a growing participation in the social consciousness and a sense of the common worth of things. . . ." Without keeping play alive, adults become ill at ease with goalless activity and tend to play very little. This is why mystics like Meister Eckhart insist that we learn to "live without a why, love without a why, and work without a why." Play and art seem to be almost synonymous in children who often report feeling colors, seeing tones, and hearing visual patterns. A kind of magical significance occurs for them as they play. Thus Howard Gardner concludes that "we should think of play as a necessary antecedent for participation in the aesthetic process."

Carl Jung felt that creativity comes from play and fantasy. He is right. The true artist plays with his or her tools, inspiration, intuition, forms, colors, musical instruments, even mind. Play takes us to realms that are preconscious and prejudgmental. Let judgment happen later, after the play. Give play its due. In play, our imaginations not only get refreshed, they also get set up to connect with new and untried possibilities. Play is the mother of surprise. Surprise is a sure sign of Spirit at play, Spirit at work.

11. Stay Close to the Prerational

Part of play, part of honoring the child within us all, is to stay near to that which precedes the rational. A long litany of experiences can be spelled out that qualify as "prerational." Among them are the following:

music
theater
painting
sculpture
comedy, humor
dance
drumming
ritual
the earth
the sea
the trees
the animals
the birds
sexuality
ritual
art of any kind
nature of any kind
  (other than human nature)

laughter
folly
the body
all that gives rise to wonder

Otto Rank felt that the biggest failing of our civilization (and also that which brought down the Roman Empire) was our excessive rationalization. He felt that the future of soul itself was the future of our choosing what I call the "prerational" to the rational. Only this would inspire and ignite our powers of creativity, powers that if gone unused lead to neuroses and addictions of all kinds on a grand scale. And powers that if used wisely could carry our species to its next stage of evolution, indeed to the next stage of the meaning of soul.

To combat rationalism it is best to reimmerse ourselves in the prerational. When we do that we can bring what we learn to the table of the rational and make a genuine, not a bogus, contribution. What lies at the level of the prerational unites us much more than it divides us. The rational divides, indeed it learns by separation, distance, and naming. The prerational brings together. It creates community and bonding, and it melts barriers between peoples.

The indigenous peoples were and still are experts at the prerational. Their wisdom and insight were not based on rationalism but on experience and on the handed-down experience of elders and storytellers and ceremonies—all of which united them to the world and forces that were far greater than the human. Their imaginations were kindled by matching wits with the animal, plant, and sky kingdoms. They fought collective amnesia, the loss of memory that more modern tribes so easily fall into. They kept traditions alive and for a purpose. Collective memory and morphic resonance were tapped into by their ritual and their love of ancestors.

Maria Montessori observed how special work with the hands is for human beings. "All men will resemble one another in the way they use their feet. But no one can tell what any given man will do with his hands. . . . The hand is in direct connect with man's soul . . . and in the light of history we see it connected with the development of civilization. . . . If men had used only speech to communicate their thought, no traces would remain of past generations. . . . When a free spirit exists, it aches to materialize itself in some form of work, and for this the hands are needed. Everywhere we find traces of men's handiwork, and through these we catch a glimpse of his spirit."

12. Pray by Calling on the Muses and Associate with Other Artists Who Do the Same

Plato taught that "memory is the mother of the Muses." If he is correct, then when we exercise our memories by calling on the ancestors, the communion of saints, the communion of beauty-makers and truth-tellers and artists, we will conjure up the arrival of the Muses. Memory lies at the heart of all ritual. Rabbi Heschel says all of Jewish worship can be summarized in one word: "Remember." And "Zikr," the basis of Sufi ritual, means "to remember." Christians invoke Jesus' words, "Do this in memory of me," when they gather to worship. Thus when we come together to do ritual we are involved in deep and collective remembering. We are also involved in calling upon the Muses because memory calls in the Muses.

But just who are the Muses? They are those beings, living and dead, who assist us in our creativity. Interestingly, the word "muse" comes from the same Greek root word that gives us the words "music" and "mysticism," "museum" and "myth." The Muses and an awakened mysticism come together. The word "mysticism" means, among other things, to "enter the mysteries" and to "shut off the senses." It is often important to shut down the senses for a while in order to journey more deeply into the mysteries. Writer Jan Phillips reports that "I believe that the moment I open to the gifts of the Muse, I open myself to the Creation. And become one with the Mother of Life Itself."

If Carl Jung is correct when he says that creativity comes from the realm of the mothers, then whatever gets us to the realm of the mothers is allowing our creativity to flow. If opening up to the Muses makes us "one with the Mother of Life itself," it is an exercise to engage in. Highly recommended. By honoring Divinity as the goddess, as Wisdom, as Mother, we are putting distance between ourselves and an all-male patriarchy, which does not respect the powers of creativity and imagination but would rather control them at all costs. Remembering the naming of "God as Mother" is one way to put us more into the realm of the mothers, the matrix of creativity itself. Call on God as Mother, and the Spirit of Creativity will find a place in one's heart and heart-work. Frederick Turner called indigenous religion a religion of "aboriginal mother love," one more reason why the resurrection of indigenous spirituality in our time is a powerful source for reawakening creativity in all of us.

Let the struggle of other artists support you in your struggle. Develop imaginations together. Read the biographies and autobiographies of artists to learn what their lives are really like. Ask them questions. Seldom have I found artists to have an easy life. Those who find balance of an interior kind have often found it at a great price: by living as hermits for a while; by honoring their own mistakes; by admitting when they have trusted too much or gone too far; by taking risks and sometimes failing. The artist's life is not an easy one, especially in a culture that respects creativity less than it does competition and rationality.

13. Practice Intimacy

Artists must know something about intimacy and practice familiarity with their tools as well as their images and the recipients of their images. A painter must be able to look into the soul of the person he or she is painting. A musician asleep at night receives visitations from Muses and angels of song. The artist must pursue subject-subject relationships more than subject-object ones.

Gaston Bachelard believes that we first learn intimacy

from enclosed spaces and that this learned intimacy serves to develop our imaginative powers. "The gentle warmth of enclosed regions is the first indication of intimacy. The warm intimacy is the root of all images." He links intimacy with immensity. In other words, the awe we experience when we encounter the grandness of the cosmos is both an *intense* and an *intimate* experience. This is how he puts it: "Immensity in the intimate domain is intensity, an intensity of being, the intensity of a being evolving in a vast perspective of intimate immensity. . . . Grandeur progresses in the world in proportion to the deepening of intimacy. . . . Slowly, immensity becomes a primal value, a primal, intimate value." In the presence of immensity, we become "liberated from [our] cares and thoughts, even from [our] dreams. One is no longer shut up in his weight, the prisoner of his own being."

Solitude is a part of this encounter with immensity because "immensity is within ourselves. It is attached to a sort of expansion of being that life curbs and caution arrests, but which starts again when we are alone. As soon as we become motionless, we are elsewhere; we are dreaming in a world that is immense." This call to solitude might be construed as a call to meditation, which takes us into solitude. So central is grandeur to our souls for Bachelard that he says that "immensity becomes conscious of itself, through man." A human is a "vast being" wherein the word "vast" evokes calm, peace, and serenity. We were made for vastness. That is why peace and rest follow when we encounter it. This is like Thomas Aquinas saying every human soul is "capax universi," capable of the universe. We are restless without the universe as part of our souls. Bachelard speaks of a "dual universe of the cosmos and the depths of the human spirit."

Psyche and cosmos go together but in an altogether intimate manner. Thomas Berry points out that intimacy was characteristic of the Native peoples' relationship to the bioregion in which they dwelled. To survive—to find the animals, the water, the shelter necessary for survival—indigenous people relied on intimacy with the land. Intimacy is about survival. Berry writes: "Nothing escapes the role of intimacy. There is such a thing as considering the curvature of space as an intimacy of the universe with every being in the universe." Intimacy is reciprocal. "The region responds to the attention it receives from the various members of the community."

When we practice intimacy we are developing our powers of imagination and creativity. When we ignore intimacy we are contributing to the powers of destruction. As Barry Lopez puts it, "The land, virtually powerless before political and commercial entities, finds itself finally with no defenders. It finds itself bereft of intimates with indispensable, concrete knowledge." We are those intimates. We are those artists so in love with land and existence itself that we defend the land and stand up for it. We pay a price because we are so in love. Artists teach us that: to love what we give birth to and to love those with whom we give birth. Co-creation makes us lovers on a bigger scale than ever imagined.

Look for the evidence of creativity and art in the non-human world, for it can keep us creative when the human world is fighting our creativity or trying to control it. Continually drink in the evidence of how creative our universe is and how its compulsion to give birth is everywhere. This is support for our own creative souls and work.

At the level of our interpersonal relationships, we practice intimacy and often encounter Muses in the process. Many are the artists who found not only friendship and love but a Muse-connection in their friends or lovers. We sometimes draw our deepest and richest creativity from one another. It is important to acknowledge this and honor it and be grateful for it. Sometimes the attraction between two people takes place at the level of Muse-enhancing. Spirit speaks through two human beings as well as to humans from other beings and other realms. Being alert is key. And being thankful is to be expected.

If Muses exist in our everyday life, then it is a good idea to hang out with Muse-like people when we can. Invite an artist over for dinner. Hang out with artists. Attend their shows, honor and support them. Dr. Estés observes that "creativity is not a solitary movement. That is its power. Whatever is touched by it, whoever hears it, sees it, senses it, knows it, is fed. That is why beholding someone else's creative word, image, idea, fills us up, inspires us to our own creative work."

14. *Meditate and Develop a Spiritual Practice*

Intimacy can be learned from solitude, and meditation can teach us to be home with solitude. How will we bring in the spiritual if we are not emptied and open to the Spirit?

Dr. Estés, like Eckhart, compares creativity to a flowing river, "the river beneath the river, which flows and flows into our lives." But to flow in, there must be an *in*, a space that the river can fill. "The creative force flows over the terrain of our psyches looking for the natural hollows, the *arroyos*, the channels that exist in us." We don't do the filling, we just do the emptying which is the preparing.

How will we become emptied and open to the Spirit without some spiritual practice? Meditation allows us to voluntarily prepare for the coming of the Spirit by bringing together all our attention and powers of focusing. Eckhart, as we have seen, compares this gathering and focusing of our minds to the apostles at the time of Pentecost. They were "gathered together" in the Upper Room, and because they were gathered together the Spirit was able to come in a big way.

So it is with us. When we gather our thoughts, feelings, our wandering and chattering minds into one place and focus our attention, we are meditating. We are calming the mind, heart, and imagination, and this prepares us for the creativity that can then flow to us and through us. Thich Nhat Hanh defines "meditation" as "stopping, calming, and looking deeply." There is a need in our lives, and in our creative lives in particular, to stop, calm, and look deeply. The key to meditation, as Thich Nhat Hanh sees it, is "to be in the present moment, to be aware that we are here and now; that the only moment to be alive is the present moment." In other words, to put the past totally out of our mind, and the future totally out of our mind, for just a while so that the present can receive its full attention from us. Just to be. Out of the being will come the creativity. Out of the being will come tomorrow and the future. But we must attain this level of being first. And when we do attain it, good things will result: joy and openness to the Spirit, among them. "When we are mindful, touching deeply the present moment, we can see and listen deeply, and the fruits are always understanding, acceptance, love, and the desire to relieve suffering and bring joy." Thus by meditating we come to the goal of all our art and creativity; we are in the presence of the via transformativa, which pulls and directs our creativity to its most useful end: compassion and joy.

The word "mindfulness" that is so common in Buddhist practice names an important observance for any artist. Who would not want to tap into his or her mind in order to use it in its fullness? Who does not want to be filled with imagination and good thoughts, with fresh fruit and new ideas to give birth to? But "mindfulness" requires "mindemptiness." That is the role of meditation: to so empty the mind that fullness can occur, that newness can enter, that Spirit can flow.

Dr. Clarissa Estés uses the example of the wolf in the wild when speaking of our need to focus. "When wolves perceive pleasure or danger, they first become utterly still.

They become like statues, utterly focused so they can see, so they can hear, so they can sense what is *there*, sense what is there in its most elemental form." We, too, want to return to the "elemental form" of things. The Wild Woman also focuses: "This is what Wild Woman offers us: the ability to see what is before us through focusing, through stopping and looking and smelling and seeing and feeling and tasting. Focusing is the use of all of our senses, including intuition. It is from this world that women come to claim their own voices, their own values, their imaginations. . . . If you've lost focus, just sit down and be still. . . . You need do no more."

There are many spiritual practices to assist us in focusing and emptying the mind, meditating and connecting us to Spirit. One whole genre is found in what we call in our educational programs "art as meditation." Art as meditation is simply entering into the artistic process *not* to produce a work of art but to *be with the process*. By focusing on the process and not the product, we are detoxing art from being merely a production or an exercise in technique and are returning to the mind's work itself. A side effect of this practice is that very often one discovers in art as meditation how much art one has inside one. But that is a side effect. The purpose is to discover the being inside the artist. And this happens time and again. Art as meditation also gets one into healthy habits of realizing how one's work can be itself a meditation practice if entered into with that attitude in mind. Speaking of my own experience, I often "get lost" and get calmed while writing or while preparing a lecture or while lecturing. Not always, but often enough to keep me going, I have deep spiritual experiences *while working*. This is art as mediation also. Art as meditation is about bringing all your powers to bear on the art work at hand. There is no limit to the kind of art work. It may be drumming or dancing, singing or painting, working clay or sculpting wood, massaging, or creating altars. All these works and more we offer at our schools of spirituality. I tell the students that it really doesn't matter which one you choose to take—the results can be the same in any meditation practice.

One of the many gifts that are available to us today because of the coming together of cultures on an unprecedented scale is a wide array of meditation practices from spiritual traditions the world over. Andrew Harvey has done us a great favor in gathering many of them in his fine and useful book, *The Direct Path*. The following are a few of the practices he recommends that seem especially useful for developing the artist in us all. One practice is to find a quiet place and a healthy posture and dedicate the meditation practice to the liberation of all sentient beings. Chanting "OM" is, in fact, chanting "A-U-M." Three sounds are involved—ah, oo, and mm. It is believed that this is the sound "that the Godhead 'makes' when and as It creates reality." What a fine meditation—to enter into the Divine creative sound. Millions of cells in our bodies awaken by the vibratory sound. Then rest in the joy and peace that follow the chanting.

A second practice is to chant the word "MA." This invokes the presence of the Divine Mother who "permeates the Creation at every level and draws every sentient being in the Creation always to its breast." This chant is meant to be done softly and with a long, drawn-out syllable. By combining this chant with the OM chant in one session, a balance of energy will be felt.

A third practice is what Harvey calls a "simple meditation." Simply sitting and breathing and letting all thoughts go—not attacking them but letting them go, observing them in a detached way if they come up. This is called "awareness that does not think." Harvey comments: "Eventually you will discover, if you practice meditation 'with pure intention and firm determination,' that you will be able when life presents you with great pain or difficulty to 'see' them from a position of peaceful detachment; this will not dissolve either the difficulty or the pain but will enable you to remain creative within them, free from their worst ravages." It keeps you in touch with the Divine inside.

It is important, indeed vital, at this moment in cultural and planetary history that humans learn to calm ourselves and to call on our best and most positive natures. For this reason, it is essential that we learn to meditate and to teach our children to meditate. Meditation is simply one more way to use the mind. To ignore it is to ignore a great aspect of our mind, an aspect that feeds peace and feeds creativity.

There is a further, scientific reason for meditation as well. We now understand that we humans possess three brains: the reptilian brain (or crocodile brain), which has been around the longest—for three or four hundred million years; the mammal brain; and the human/intellectual brain. The reptilian brain operates our sexuality and our respiratory system and our fight/flight reaction responses. Crocodiles are quite well known for their win/lose mentality. Reptiles do not bond, even with their own children. Therefore it is important that we humans get to appreciate our crocodile brains but not allow ourselves to be overrun by them. Reptilian energy, win/lose, is everywhere evident in the human scene today. How do we control it?

I see two options. The first was offered by the western Christian myths of St. George or of St. Martin of Tours slaying the dragon. I do not think that is a good idea. We do not want to slay the reptile in us (after all, this brain runs our sexual response as well as other responses).

The second option comes from the East: Dance with the dragon; honor the dragon. I would say, pet the dragon. And this is where meditation comes in. Meditation calms the reptilian brain in us, putting it at rest. We know this from observing crocodiles—they love to sleep in the sun. Alone very often, they are capable of great solitude. Meditation also teaches us to be at home with solitude. I believe Buddha's genius was in putting a leash on the crocodile. We all need to do that. We all need meditation practices today.

When we can calm the reptilian brain in us, then the other brains can assert themselves more energetically. The mammal brain introduces compassion to the world in a tactile way. Mammals bond and mammals touch. Mammals have wombs, and the word "compassion" comes from the word for "womb" in both Hebrew and Arabic. But chimpanzee and gorilla populations, we have learned, are limited in their compassion to their own tribe. They are not compassionate beyond their tribe.

Thus it is the most recent brain, that of the human/intellectual kind, that has the task of *expanding our capacity for compassion*. This might explain why so many spiritual teachers from so many spiritual traditions—Jesus and Buddha, Isaiah and Muhammad, Black Elk and Mahatma Gandhi and Dr. King—all teach compassion. But for compassion to be unleashed on a global scale we must all learn first to tame the crocodile brain and to honor the mammal brain. That is what meditation does for us. We cannot ignore it.

The most creative people among us are often beset by drama and forces of guilt, doubt, darkness, and fear. They are often highly sensitive, and this can be a burden as well as a blessing. Vulnerability is a necessary part of their lifestyle—they must wear a thin veil between themselves and life itself in order to represent life and report back on it. Oscar Wilde observed that "life breaks everybody." If that is true, it is especially true of artists who dance so closely with life's dangers in order to tell the truth about it.

It is for this reason that many artists are tempted by stimulants of alcohol or drugs—sometimes to "come down" from their highs, sometimes to just "get some sleep," and sometimes with wishes of being inspired by seemingly unattainable Muses. I believe that the future invites artists to let go of these outside stimulants that so easily become addictions and to commit to meditation instead. To train the mind to do its own letting go and relaxing allows the Muses freer access to our souls and work.

What happens in meditation is what happens in our acts of creativity: We become united with the Divine Spirit, which is the Spirit of Creation and Creativity. Our sixth chakras become dwelling places for the Divine. We con-temple there, that is, we share a sacred temple with the Divine. We call it "contemplation" or unity or forgetfulness of separation and duality. And then creativity surely flows. Meister Eckhart puts it this way: "The eye in which I see God is the same eye in which God sees me. My eye and God's eye are one eye and one seeing and one knowing and one loving."

15. Deepen Our Sense of Gratitude

If Otto Rank is correct when he defines the artist as one who wants to leave behind a gift, and if all of us are artists in some way, then we all want to leave behind a gift. Why do we want to do this? Only, it seems to me, if we have tasted deeply enough of life's blessings that we want to say "thank you" by offering others their chance at life. We leave gifts behind because we are full of thanks, and we must say "thank you."

Why are we so full of thanks? Because we have developed our awareness of our receptivity and we have come to realize that all this glory of which we are a part—time and space, light and dark, creation and its fourteen-billion-year history, earth and its wonders, nature and its magnificent imagination and artistry, our own species and its accomplishments for good and ill, our families, loved ones, and lovers—is a gift. A gift implies a Gift-giver.

In leaving gifts behind, we are imitating the Divine Gift-giver, the Creator, who has left us so many gifts. Eckhart says that "it is God's nature to give big gifts. And for this reason, the more valuable the gifts are, the more does God give of them." The gifts we give come from deep within us. Indeed, they are alive there! "There all things are present, living and seeking within the soul what is spiritual, where they are in their best and highest meaning." In Eckhart's opinion, God needs to bestow the gifts of creativity upon us, and we have a responsibility to be receptive. If we are not, if we reject the gifts of the Creative Spirit, then we are guilty of violence to God. "It is God's nature to make gifts, and his being depends on making gifts to us if we are down below. If we are not here, and if we receive nothing, we act violently toward him and we kill him. If we cannot do this to him, we are still doing it to ourselves and being violent as far as we are concerned." It is when we have become detached from time and space that the "Father sends his Son into the soul." This Son is the Cosmic Christ, the Divine Wisdom or Sophia, the Logos, the Word. Gratitude begets more grace and beauty. Gratitude begets co-creation.

Recently my next-door neighbor's plumbing sprung a leak, and her water was turned off for five days. These five days constituted a lesson in *not taking water for granted*. We can all choose from time to time some voluntary simplicity and voluntary letting go by way of fasting from something we take for granted. This is how to increase our sense of gratitude for what is.

There are times when I sit down to write at my computer and a simple prayer comes to my mind. It is the prayer that we said for table grace when I was a child. "Bless us O Lord and these thy gifts which we are about to receive through Christ our Lord. Amen." This grace before the meal of creativity becomes a kind of prelude to my creative work. Like eating, we are about to receive graces from the universe and its Maker. Why not utter a prayer of gratitude, a grace before the meal of writing a book (or any other creative work)? Who knows who will be joining us for the ongoing feast long after we are gone from the table?

{eight}

where do we go from here? putting creativity to work in culture and everyday life

 Awakening imagination can arouse our creativity to solve problems and move our species to its next level of evolutionary development. In her book, with the stirring title of *Imagine Inventing Yellow*, poet, potter, and painter M. C. Richards defines "imagination" and hints at its consequences: "Imagination means singing to a wide invisible audience. It means receptivity to the creative unconscious, the macrocosmic mind, artistic mind. It makes erotic philosophers of us, as we imagine the world in images that make whole. To imagine is to give birth to—to embody the Spirit in word and picture and behavior. The world will change when we can imagine it different and, like artists, do the work of creating new social forms."

Let us consider four areas where arousing the "artistic

mind" can heal and transform our species today, leading it
to its fuller potential.

1. Education

Our species is unique because we so desperately require the
learning that education brings us. Other species are far more
programmed by their DNA than we are. We go to school or
to elders to learn. How are we doing?

There exists an educational crisis all over the planet. Indeed, it can be said that education is in chaos. The main reason is that we have a clash of three worlds happening at
once: The modern world and its educational agenda is coming up against the postmodern world with its unique needs
and agenda, and in many parts of the world this is also rub-
bing up against the premodern world with its educational
agenda. An example of the latter is the indigenous peoples
of Africa, the Americas, and Asia. In America, this encounter
is felt fiercely in inner-city schools where so many of the
populations come from indigenous backgrounds, be they
African Americans with African sensibilities, Hispanic Americans with pre-Columbian indigenous sensibilities, Native
American students with theirs, or Asian Americans with
their own ingrained cultural and familial educational backgrounds. It is clear that our school systems are often failing
to meet the needs of these students. Their drop-out rates
are alarming and do not seem to be receding. Instead of education providing a rite of passage into adulthood and an
access into the dominant culture's opportunities at work, the

educational experience seems to be a big part of the problem. Gangs seem to provide more of what many youngsters yearn for than do classes.

Why is this? I believe it is because the premodern cultures—African, American, Asian—valued creativity as being the heart and soul of education. Storytelling and ceremony, myths that tell the great stories of how we got here and why we are here and what, therefore, our common ethic can be—these comprised the basis of education for tens of thousands of years for our species. The modern European agenda is a recent agenda. It allowed us to conquer the earth and subdue many peoples and cultures, but it did not teach us *survival*, that is, sustainability, with the earth and her processes. It did not teach us ethics or aesthetics. It did not teach us reverence or gratitude. It did not teach us wonder, it did not keep the child, which is wisdom herself, alive in us. Indeed, it banished wisdom at the expense of raw knowledge.

That raw knowledge devoid of wisdom is now coming back to haunt us all in the form of what Thomas Berry dares to call the "reflective barbarianism" of modern academia, where posturing and criticizing can continue ad infinitum while the world burns all around us. As Berry warns, "Most of the damage on the planet is happening at the hands of people with PhDs." Here is a warning, if ever there was one, of a misdirected educational project. Knowledge without wisdom is dangerous.

In addition, a soul-loss is occurring in the name of education. When learning loses its sense of joy, its sense of wonder and delight, when exams and competition replace wonder as the sole motivation for working hard in school, when the sense of the sacredness of learning is forgotten, then education is a failure and is doomed to fail. All the money the federal government or others pump into such a system will not save it. Education requires a deeper healing than we dare imagine. I see that healing occurring in four steps: Cosmology, Kenosis (Emptying), Creativity and Compassion.

1. Cosmology

We need to bring the universe back to university and then to all our professional schools and all our educational systems, from grade school through graduate school. Only a sense of the wisdom of the cosmos and the earth can generate wisdom and excitement in the learning heart and mind of the human being. Only when we know our place in the universe can we know our place in society, family, and our profession. Today's new creation story as understood through science needs to be required study for all learners at every level of learning. Maria Montessori understood the importance of cosmology for children when she wrote: "If the idea of the universe would be presented to the child in the right way, it will create in him admiration and wonder.... The stars, earth, stones, life of all kinds form a whole in relation with each other, and so close is this relation that we cannot understand a stone without some understanding of the great sun! The child begins to ask, 'How did it come into being, and how will it end?' 'What am I?' 'What is our task in this wonderful universe?' 'Do we merely live here for ourselves or is there something more for us to do?'"

Cosmology is an integral part of what the young soul is yearning to learn—and the more dangerous the circumstances, the more one is stretched to ask questions about the cosmos: Why are we here? Who is here with us? Is life worth the struggle? A woman who worked for seventeen years in South Central Los Angeles with inner-city kids told me that she has never known a group of people who were more curious or interested in cosmology than those kids. But were the public schools teaching it? How can they if the educators themselves have been deprived of learning it?

2. Kenosis, or Emptying

School must be a place where we can learn the vast space and emptiness of our minds. We need to learn to study nothingness as well as somethingness. The traditional word for learning the emptiness and nothingness of our minds is "meditation." If that word is a stumbling block, we can put our poets to work to find other names, for example "mental gym" or what Maria Montessori called "making silence." She sets a time aside every day in her classes for youngsters, which is a time for "making silence." This practice should be included in every curriculum from kindergarten through graduate school. Our species needs to honor silence, to let it in, yes, to "make silence." This is the taming of the reptilian brain that we spoke of in the last chapter. We cannot survive as a species—and probably not as individuals either—without making silence.

Montessori developed a "silence game" whose purpose was not to bring order to a noisy classroom but to encourage the meditative spirit of the child. One child during the "silence game" reported hearing "spring coming"; another, "the voice of God speaking inside me." Comments Montessori: "Silence often brings us the knowledge which we had not fully realized, that we possess within ourselves an interior life. The child by means of silence sometimes becomes aware of this for the first time."

What about adults? I know an instructor in Tai Chi who tells me that when he teaches in prisons many of the most violent inmates there tell him that this is the "first time in their lives" that they have ever experienced silence. Isn't silence necessary to counteract violence? Are adults learning to "make silence" and thereby becoming empowered to teach youngsters how to do it? Comments one educator: "Silence predisposes the soul for certain inner experiences. You are not the same after silence as you were before it. It is one of the tragedies of our mechanical age that so many people grow up without ever having discovered the beauty of silence."

Instead, we have in America today the perverse situation wherein adults are drugging our children so they will sit still in the classroom. Adults are reaping great financial rewards by doing so. Adultism reigns. Our depraved and demonic imaginations have made up two diseases, one called ADD, Attention Deficit Disorder, and the other ADHD, the "hyperactive" version of the same. The first issue that should be raised about this so-called disease is our diets. We live in a culture that is making profits on kids by putting sugar and sugar-making carbohydrates into everything children eat, such as cereal and soft drinks, in such quantities that we are encouraging nervousness and broad ranges of mood swings on their part. We are also planting seeds for diabetes and for obesity.

Dr. Fred Baughman, a pediatrician for thirty-five years, says that "ADD is not a real disease, but rather a contrived illusion, a marketplace tool." The "cure" for this supposed disease is Ritalin, a brainchild of the pharmaceutical giant Ciba-Geigy. Ciba makes millions of dollars annually with this drug aimed at rendering children more obedient in the classroom. Over 10 percent of American schoolchildren have been diagnosed with ADD, and the number has doubled every four years. In some classrooms, over half the kids are on Ritalin. In Texas, a class-action lawsuit has been launched against Ciba because Ciba gave $748,000 to promote Ritalin to parents, doctors, and educators "to increase the market for its product," according to the lawsuit. What happens to children who are put on drugs at an early age because they are distracted or fidgety in school? Their education becomes an education in drug taking. Drugs will cure anything, they are told. What happens when they get older can only be guessed at—Prozac is next and then, no doubt, Viagra.

Ritalin can squelch imagination and spontaneity in children, rendering them docile and servile. As Rex Weyler has put it, "Children labeled with 'attention deficit' and then drugged become more amenable to the rote, boring tasks dominating our schoolrooms. 'Attention deficit' simply means the kids aren't paying attention to what the teachers are doing. I don't believe the problem is with the kids or their ability to be attentive. I've seen kids diagnosed with ADD show extraordinary powers of attention when their imagination has been stimulated. The real problem—the problem that is masked by these fanciful 'disorders' and drugs—is an Imagination Deficit Disorder within our school system."

Yes! He is right. As long as we ignore the imagination of the cosmos in our classrooms, we will have an Imagination Deficit Disorder. Anthropocentrism always leads to boredom. That is what is haunting our school systems. Educators must learn the new cosmology or become drug pimps to the youngsters. And to learn the new cosmology educators themselves must learn to "make silence" in order to take in the big and beautiful news. They must learn kenosis as we all must learn kenosis.

Not just Ritalin but Adderall, Metadate CD, and other drugs are being advertised directly to parents. This represents a totally new trend in advertising, since previously only doctors were approached by the drug companies. "Last year, doctors wrote almost 20 million monthly prescriptions for the stimulants. . . . most of those prescriptions were written for children, especially boys. The drugs had sales last year of $758 million, 13 percent more than in 1999." The *Journal of the American Medical Association* reports a "disturbing" increase in the number of stimulants aimed at children under five, "most of whom are too young, according to the drugs' labels, to take them."

3. Creativity

Creativity is in all of us. If education means to "lead out of" (from the Latin *educere*), then it is the primary task of school to lead creativity out of every child. It is *not* the task of school to tell youngsters that they can't draw or can't sing or can't dance. Technique and awareness of the unique gifts students have come later. First is to instill the confidence, trust, and ultimately the courage it will take every human being to live with chaos and transform it, to live with creativity and honor it. If education fails at this, it fails at its most important task.

As we discussed in chapter 2, it is of the essence of being human to be creative. Why then are our educational models not built on awakening and eliciting *that which is most human* out of us? *Why isn't all education an education in creativity? An education in the essence of being human?* The education of the future must be of this sort. We have no other option. The political debates about education seem to me to be based on promises of who can promise the most tests and exams of our youngsters. I don't think this is the radical rebeginning of education that our youngsters need and deserve.

Rather, we could totally reinvent education by centering it on 1) cosmology and 2) creativity. They obviously fit like hand and glove since integral to the new cosmology is the awareness of how profoundly creative the universe is and has been for its entire fourteen billion years. Can we teach creativity? Yes, insofar as we provide the nonjudgmental space for it to flow and hold it up as a supreme ethical value. This we have called "art as meditation," but it can just as well be called "art practice" or "aesthetics in action," or some other euphemism that distinguishes these art classes from being object-oriented, keeping the focus on art as process, not art as product. Nonjudgment is key. Creativity does not need thought police at its earliest stages (if at all). Let imagination flow daily in our classrooms, and you will find that the fidgeting that we diagnose as ADD will melt quickly.

We also teach creativity by recognizing its omnipresence in nature all around us—this gives permission to students to tap into the earth imagination and the cosmos imagination and, ultimately, the Creator's imagination. Studying the works and lives of artists is another way to alert and inspire and even to warn students of the powers of imagination for good or ill. Sharing the myths from Prometheus to Adam and Eve to Jesus and others is also part of such a curriculum of creativity. Sharing the ecstasy of the mystics and the gift of imagination also contributes to the excitement of it all.

Creativity is fun. There ought to be no fear of fun in the

classroom. Fun belongs everywhere in a postmodern time. The more dire the times, the more we need fun in our lives and culture. By letting imagination in, we are letting fun in. When fun returns, fantasy finds its healthy place, options are put before us, possibilities return. Hope happens, for hope is about the possible, while despair is about the impossible. Creativity banishes despair—at least for a while. An education in creativity will bring about hope if not optimism.

I have been involved in education as a student, a teacher, and an administrator for the past fifty-five years of my life. I have had the privilege of studying in Europe, as well as in America, and teaching on other continents as well. I have to say the following: In learning, there lies some of the sweetest, most ecstatic, wildest, and most sacred times of my life. I resist and resent educational structures that remove the sacred and the fun and the good times, the awe and the joy, from the spiritual experience of learning. Wherever this is happening, it needs to be remedied. Thomas Aquinas taught that "the proper object of the heart is truth and justice." Everyone enjoys learning. Learning is to our mind and heart what eating is to our stomachs: delectable and delicious— *provided that* educators, like good chefs, present learning that is healthy, hearty, and beautifully prepared.

But do we? Is education doing its job? How can it if it ignores cosmology and creativity? I believe the bottom line is this: centering our education on creativity. Psychologist Abraham Maslow saw it this way: "Creative art education may be especially important, not so much for turning out artists or art products, as for turning out better people. . . . If we hope for our children that they will become full human beings, and that they will move toward actualizing the potentialities that they have, then the only kind of education that has . . . such goals is art education." The television addictions that we foist on our young people are having a profoundly deleterious effect on the development of their own imaginations. Teacher after teacher tell me that they see less and less imagination in the young people they encounter in the classroom and on the playground. Joseph Pearce warns us about the situation when he says that "the major damage of television has little to do with content: Its damage is neurological. . . . Television floods the infant-child brain with images at the very time his or her brain is supposed to learn to make images from within."

A few years ago a woman from Ohio approached me at a lecture I was giving and told me this story. A judge in her city had begged her to invent a high school where he could send tough teen-age kids, who were dropping out of the public school and getting in trouble—"an alternative to jail" was his request. She told me she was reading my books at that time, and she launched a school based *entirely on creativity.* From nine in the morning to four in the afternoon the students engaged in painting, music, poetry, rap, video, theater, dance, storytelling. What happened? First, the students showed up everyday. They often stayed after hours and begged the instructors to do the same. Second, they found a language for their anger and their hurt and their dreams. Third, after a while, they started asking questions about history, geography, Shakespeare, algebra.

The tougher the circumstances a young person has growing up, the more imagination and creativity are the key to his or her healing and empowerment. Montessori came to realize that children who behaved badly did so "because they lived in conditions in which their spirituality could not express itself. Their spirits rebelled in violence, withdrawal, selfishness and disregard for others." Lily Yeh is a prophet of our time who has chosen to work in the inner city of Philadelphia and start a center called "The Village of Arts and Humanities." There she gets community members to create artwork from the refuse around them. The results are amazing. Drug addicts have been turned around and taken leadership roles. Ages come together, and hope returns. Yeh has also worked in villages in Africa.

All schools should reinvent themselves around creativity. Then we would truly be transforming education and, hopefully, preparing ourselves to transform other aspects of community healing, living, and livelihood.

4. Compassion

What is this hope that returns when cosmology, kenosis, and creativity are engaged in the name of education? The hope is a hope in our possibility to make changes, to be instruments of transformation, to heal the planet and ourselves. To reinvent our professions so that they truly *serve* and don't *desecrate*. So that they ennoble and don't take away from the beauty and wealth of the planet for future generations. True compassion is justice, and justice requires study; it requires knowing the effects of our actions and decisions on other people—those different from ourselves—and on other beings. That is why cosmology or "local ecology" is so important for effective compassion.

Consider, for example, this one act of creativity on our parts: the building of the Grand Coulee Dam fifty years ago. Did we, in our eagerness to harness energy, take into account the suffering of other beings? A new book by David James Duncan points out that *in one day* this dam destroyed the entire population of the upper Columbia Pacific salmon—"the salmon of eastern British Columbia, a third of Washington State, and northern Idaho." Comments Duncan: "This is too easy to say: it is crucial to imagine it. Hundreds of crucial salmon strains, ancient as gods, doomed to annihilation in a day. Tens of thousands of people thrown out of sustainable outdoor work and forced to rote factory jobs. Scores of indigenous tribes impoverished if they were lucky, destroyed and dispersed if they weren't." That is the power of a single dam. America has seventy-five thousand of them.

2. Everyday Life and Relationships, Including Sexual Ones

Creativity begins at home. That is where we sleep, dress, eat, prepare for work, recover from work, get to know our kids, and communicate with those dearest to us. In all the endeavors of home life, creativity can play a major role. (Of course its opposite, passivity, can also take over, as is the case if we become addicted to television, for example.) M. C. Richards puts it this way: "By example and practice, I try to teach that creativity is built in—like the sun—it shines in everything we are and do—Look!" Does creativity shine in everything we are and do? Let us look.

I was recently having breakfast outdoors by the ocean at a retreat center, and at my table were two women commenting on how wonderful it was to eat outdoors by the water. In their conversation they came to realize that, living in the city as each of them did, they had each designed a backyard with flowing water, an indoors with pictures of nature and flowing water, and plants and more.

We sometimes underestimate how creative we are at home. Who says "I am not creative?" Every plant we care for, every picture on our wall, every color we choose for walls or furniture, the arrangement of things in a room—all this is our creativity at work. Get to it! It is not about the amount of money we spend but about the imagination we bring to the task of creating a space that is beautiful and encouraging to our home companions. We are teaching aesthetics everyday (or its opposite).

Then there are meals. How we eat, what we eat, what we refuse to eat, where we get our food, how we prepare the meal, whether we eat alone or with others, with the television on or off—all of these are creative decisions that face us in our everyday life. I am still learning much about nutrition since I was recently diagnosed with diabetes and stones in my gall bladder. My HMO wanted to take the gall bladder out, but I chose to follow a more holistic path to wholeness. The first thing I learned was about the relationship between carbohydrates, protein, and sugar. No one had ever taught me these things. Worse, no one has yet to teach the doctors at my HMO (who were so eager to take my gall bladder out) about these things. All parents, all people, should know these things. The food we take in is our primary drug, if you will. We take it three times a day. We deserve healthy food and healthy food habits. This is an art in knowing what to cook and how, what to eat and when. One lesson I am learning is that by eating five times a day (small portions) I relieve the gall bladder and pancreas so that they are happier processing the food. The result is that my sugar count, such an issue with diabetics, is going down regularly.

There is conversation. All talking is an act of creativity, as David Paladin reminds us: "If you're talking, you are being creative. You're taking concepts and changing them into words so that you can communicate with me. You're more creative than you think you are." In addition to being a painter, Paladin worked as a police chaplain. Often he had to deliver death notices to peoples' loved ones or to work with people contemplating suicide. He comments: "In that role I use a lot of creativity. I become an actor, because I try to sense what they need and then fulfill it. This the role of the artist, the shaman, the minister."

Then there is parenting. Is not parenting an art form? Is not parenting demanding of every ounce of creativity that is in us? Each child has their own personality, their own way in which to be addressed, their own form of communication. We adapt. We learn process-wise the art of parenting. We learn to know ourselves in the process: Children bring the best and the worst out of us. Family life is meant to keep us honest. And humble. Rules are not enough; the dance of creativity is required to sustain relationships as children grow older and themselves undergo deep changes when their experiences of life multiply and present challenges. Rollo May put it this way: "Creativity must be seen in the work of the scientist as well as in that of the artist, in the thinker as well as in the aesthetician; and one must not rule out the extent to which it is present in captains of modern technology as well as in a mother's normal relationship with her child." Mothering is itself an art form as is fathering.

Then there is our primary relationship. Marriage is not a noun; it is a verb. It is not a static box, a contract alone, but a creative act. Every day, surely every week and every season, adaptation is required to undergo both the chaos and the order of the relationship. A dance ensues. An art is required in building and maintaining any meaningful relationship— the arts of communication, verbal and non verbal, the art of expressing ourselves and our needs directly but not threateningly, the art of listening, of letting go, of forgiving, of remembering.

Sexuality is another element of our everyday relationships. Sexuality, too, need not be dull and boring. Margo Anand, in her book *The Art of Sexual Ecstasy*, teaches the lessons that lovers can learn from the ancient spiritual art of Tantra. It is telling that this tradition first sees sexuality in a *cosmic context*. "Tantra sees each human being as an organism that is part of a larger whole—the surrounding environment, the planet Earth, nature itself—in which rhythm and vibration are the unifying factors." Tantra brings together the energy of the sex drive with the energy of the nervous system and the brain as we experience ecstasy. Tantra transforms the sexual drive and refines it into ecstasy. I have known a number of persons, both heterosexual and homosexual, whose sexual lives and relationships with their partners were transformed, deepened, and even saved by Tantric sexual practices. But it does take practice and some work, and it is creative. Tantra introduces new dimensions of breathing, posture, play, and trust to sexuality and re-creates it.

Anand cautions, as all teachers of meditation do, that the issue in renewing sexuality is not willpower. In fact, willpower gets in the way. This is similar to Eckhart's saying that it is necessary to "live without a why." So it is necessary to do sex "without a why." Rather than willpower and control, Anand teaches, "it is actually a question of creating very intense experiences that are immediately followed by relaxing and letting go." Love-making is meant to be a creative act. Every time. She counsels breathing with awareness but not breathing with thoughts. Thoughts can interfere with love-making (as they can with any art process). "Making love through your thoughts is a bit like trying to do differential calculus with your genitals." It is by "combining your breathing with your imagination" that you come to your Inner Lover.

Much of Tantra's teaching of becoming a good lover depends on meditation practices, which allow the breath to take over and assist us to become an instrument of the natural spirit at work in us. Anand reports that, once you practice Tantric sex, the entire family often benefits. The practices of opening the heart and becoming more intimate and honest affect others, especially children, who often respond by "being more joyful, trusting, and relaxed themselves." Work and play can integrate more fully, and "as you become more playful, you can more fully enjoy the naturally playful spirit of children." When we get more creative in any aspect of life—including our love life—other areas will surely be affected.

We are all invited to our creativity when we have time off. Yesterday I took a stroll along the Truckee river near Reno on a hot Sunday afternoon. It was 98 degrees, but ordinary people found plenty of ways to be creative and cool. In just twenty minutes I observed the following examples of our species busy at play, busy at imagination. A mother and her seven-year-old son had made it out to a large rock in the middle of the rapidly flowing river. There they were, sunning on a rock, surrounded by the cold flowing water all around them. Their trip to shore was a bit slow, as the child kept leaning on Mom for help. But it was all part of a Sunday afternoon outing. Several families were fishing along the bank of the river with small kids playing in inlet pools of the refreshing river water. Two eleven-year-old boys—first with an inner tube and then atop an old sofa they found in the river—were floating down the waters toward the rapids. Laughing, kicking, falling off and climbing on to the old sofa which kept turning over on them. A couple with a dog—he on one river bank, she on the other—throwing a ball back and forth. Each time they missed the ball, the dog dove into the river to retrieve it, swimming the full width of the waters if he had to. Four hearty souls were playing volleyball in the 98-degree heat. Locals no doubt. A small truck, with an obnoxious tune going, was winding through the park grounds announcing ice cream for sale.

All this was happening in one corner of a park in twenty minutes spent observing on a river bank. So much creativity in one stroll, so much creativity in our species. When it's playtime, our imaginations come alive. Is there another species quite as imaginative as ours? I think not.

Another dimension to our everyday lives that deserves to be approached with a maximum of creativity is our dying. My mother died this year, and as a sister-in-law said to me: "She may have been difficult at times when it came to little things, but when it came to big things, like dying, she was a master teacher." One day when she was sick in the hospital my sister came to visit, and my mother said to her: "I was up all night and did not sleep at all." My sister said: "Why not? What is wrong with you now?" And my mother replied: "It's not that. It's that I have never died before, and I stayed up all night to figure out how to do it right." Days later, she turned to my two sisters from her hospital bed and said: "Roberta, it's a waste of your time staying here while I die— why don't you go out and do something important?" Then she turned to my other sister, saying: "Terry, it's a waste of *your* time watching me die. Why don't you do something more important?" Then she said: "Come to think of it, it's a waste of *my time* waiting here to die! How long is this going to take?"

When the priest came to deliver her last rites, my mother said to him: "Do you know who I am? I am Matthew Fox's mother. Now how many of his books have you read?" He went to the Internet that night, and when I arrived in town he had a number of theological questions to put to me based on my writings. Mom certainly turned the tables on him and chose not to receive the last rites passively.

When I came to say my farewell to my mother, our last conversation went like this. She said: "Tim, I am not afraid to die. I have lived a wonderful life. I will miss you kids, but I am ready to go." I said to her: "Mom, I bet I know why." She said: "Why?" I said: "First, you are curious. And second, you are looking forward to an adventure." She replied: "Exactly." That was her last word to me, "exactly." With that we embraced, and I went to catch my plane. She died twelve days later.

For her funeral she gave me two instructions: No crying, and she wanted rave dancing. (She was eighty-seven years old.) So we danced at her grave site—seven children with spouses and ex-spouses, seventeen grandchildren, and seventeen great grandchildren. I observed that the youngest grandchildren had been very restless at the funeral service and were missing my mother terribly. I instructed them to fill the hole in the ground where the urn with her ashes lay with hand fulls and then shovels of dirt. This exercise produced a noticeable effect in calming them down. There was a lesson in it they will carry forever: that Death is natural and a return to the earth. When we finished our group dancing, a very strong breeze came wafting directly through our circle. We all felt is was a spirit presence approving of our farewell to her.

Like my sister-in-law, I feel that my mother's dying was a very creative act and deliberately intended on her part to leave all of us with something to think about as regards our own living and dying.

Whether our everyday lives and the countless decisions they demand of us are creative or not depends most of all upon our attitude and our sense of self. We can choose or not choose to be creative. Paladin put it this way: "Look at yourself as magicians, as healers, as lovers of humanity, as givers and sharers. From that perspective living becomes an art in itself. Then everything you do becomes magic!"

3. Politics

The ecological crisis, the global-warming phenomenon, the terrorist crisis, and the energy crisis of our times are a kind of canary in our mines for us. It is a stern warning, a wake-up call, that we must put our imaginations into high gear to reinvent the way we take energy from this planet and use it. The solution is our imaginations. That is our way out.

Sometimes we forget the historical nature of our energy crisis. Our dependence on fossil fuels is really only about one hundred fifty years old. Before we enlisted oil rigs to bring the oil up from the innards of mother earth, we were highly dependent in the early part of the nineteenth century on whales. Whales were our primary source of oil. Just as we have closed our eyes in the twentieth century to the intimate relationship we have with earth in order to exploit what is inside her for our energy needs—an exploitation that has warmed up the planet and is provoking widescale extinction spasms—so in the nineteenth century we shut our eyes to the truth of who the whale was. Following is a description of the whale attitudes of that time.

Instead of seeing their prey as a fifty- to sixty-ton creature whose brain was close to six times the size of their own, the whalemen preferred to think of a whale as what one commentator called "a self-propelled tub of high-income lard." Whales were described by the amount of oil they would produce (as in a "fifty-barrel whale"). No attempt was made to regard them as anything more than a commodity whose constituent parts (head, blubber, ambergris, etc.) were of value to humans. What was the result of seeing the whale as object and not as subject? "Just as the skinned corpses of buffaloes would soon dot the prairies of the American West, so did the headless gray remains of sperm whales litter the Pacific Ocean in the early nineteenth century." Those who wrestled with whales and brought in their oil became "accustomed to the brutal business of whaling. The repetitious nature of the work—a whaler was, after all, a factory ship—tended to desensitize the men to the awesome wonder of the whale."

It is this *desensitization* to the awesome wonder of everything—life, soil, forests, sky, other species, our own bodies, earth itself—that we can no longer tolerate as a species. This is the direction we can move *from* when we shift from fossil fuels to other sources of energy.

Of the hundreds of ships that prowled the oceans in search of whales to slaughter in the year 1819, one, the *Essex*, met a unique fate. While the *Essex* was attempting to kill sperm whales in the deep Pacific, one whale turned and attacked the ship and sunk it. Its twenty-man crew took three months to row home and only eight survived, and they did so by, among other things, eating the remains of their shipmates. There is a lesson here, predicted by Hildegard of Bingen in the twelfth century, of what happens when humans exploit nature. "God will allow nature to punish humanity," she declared, if humanity interferes with the justice inherent in the "web of creation." What that whale did in turning on his exploiters almost two hundred years ago is parallel to what the ozone layer and the warming of the atmosphere are doing to our species today. One cannot damage the web of creation with impunity forever. Sooner or later we will pay the piper.

Just as we moved from whales to oil last century, so we can move from fossil fuels to solar-driven ones in the twenty-first century. It is the thing to do. We can do it because we have to do it. This is the sustainable and clean path of the future. What is holding us back is vested interests that do not want to face the future. And the lack of imagination and creativity to solve the practical problems that wind power, solar power, geothermal power, and ocean power present. It has been proposed, for example, that harnessing just 0.2 percent of the wave power in the world's oceans would provide electricity for every citizen on the planet—and it would be "clean" and renewable energy with no toxic discharges into the atmosphere. We can solve these problems and are, in fact, on the way to doing so—provided we can put the common good ahead of the good of particular corporate interests.

As for automobiles, we already have cars that travel one hundred twenty miles on one gallon of fuel. This trend can also be sustained and enlarged provided we have the commitment to imagination and creativity and provided that the common good is put ahead of the private, corporate good.

Creative economists are pointing the way to how economics can assist rather than interfere with the need for balance and economic justice between nations and peoples, environment and labor, so-called industrial and less-industrial nations. Clearly the gap between rich and poor cannot continue on its present course. Both sides suffer from the extremes of luxury excess (called "affluenza" by some), on the one hand, and destitution, on the other. The poor need and deserve to be included in economic success. Economist David Korten writes: "There is no more powerful expression of a society's values than its economic institutions. In our case, we have created an economy that values money over all else, embraces inequality as if it were a virtue, and is ruthlessly destructive of life. The tragedy is that for most of us the values of global capitalism are not our values. It is hardly surprising, therefore, that we find ourselves in psychological and social distress." And, I might add, we find ourselves watching shopping channels right up to the day we die.

This observation from Korten is not unrelated to the scourge of terrorism. It is no coincidence that terrorists are largely recruited from very poor countries. Despair breeds self-contempt, and self-contempt breeds disregard for the lives of others. (Didn't Jesus counsel that we love others as we love ourselves?) Ultimate solutions to terrorism point to a new creation of economics that is not built on greed or gluttony (consumerism) but on justice. Give us pillars of justice rather than shifting sands of "consumer confidence." Would that our economics promoted simple living with the same energy that it tries to sell consumer mania. A concerted effort to provide all in the world their basic needs is possible, but only if our economic system moves beyond consumer mania.

4. Worship

The building of strong souls and strong communities requires strong rituals—occasions that both link us to our ancestors and that speak in a language that is fresh and challenging. For five years we have been producing what we call Techno Cosmic Masses in Oakland, California, near our university in downtown Oakland. We have also sponsored these masses in Boulder, Houston, Los Angeles, Louisville, Seattle, New York City, and upstate New York. The response from both young and old alike has been powerful. I am more convinced than ever that ritual is the shortcut to unleashing creativity by telling the new creation story, healing the people through grief work, bringing joy alive, and inspiring meaning in peoples' lives. One example of the power of community grieving is the Maafa experience, in which black communities turn churches into a slave ship and relive the middle passage, burying their ancestors lost at sea during the slave trade and honoring their memories. Ritual is the natural place for artists to gather, to let go of their own wounds and ego trips, and to become gifters to the larger community.

The key to the form of our worship in the Techno Cosmic Mass is to borrow elements from rave celebrations, including dance, techno music, slides, video, and rap, and to include these in an otherwise recognizable liturgical service, which includes Eucharist and Communion. In addition, there is a strong ecumenical dimension to the service, including a Jewish rabbi or cantor singing the words of Jesus at the altar prayers and other spiritual representatives offering prayers and meditations. There is always a via negativa, or occasion for expressing grief as a group, and many people comment on how powerful this is for them. "I grieve alone in my bed-room," said one participant, "but no one ever asked me to grieve with a group before." Our species must grieve its many wrongs and hurts—from slavery to ecocide, from en-slavement of Native people to racism and adultism—if we are to release the creativity which alone can heal us. Ritual is the traditional occasion for such grieving.

The power of dance to replace sitting in pews is attested to by Dona Marimba Richards in her study on African spirit. She writes: "Through dance we experience reality as immediate to us; that is, we are identified with the uni-verse. . . . We have experienced cosmic interrelationship. . . . Dance, for us, is a religious expression. When we dance, through Rhythm, we express ourselves as cosmic beings." The fact that several African languages equate "dance" with "breathing" and "breath" with "spirit" only underscores the power of dance as prayer—a practice that indigenous people the world over recognize.

Slides, video, and rap can tell many stories that mere preaching cannot do. They arouse images in the people es-pecially when they dance. This way each participant is a "priest" or midwife of grace for himself or herself—and for one another. No one person is expected to carry the spiritual load for the rest of the group. Participation is the key. And dance guarantees participation. There is no vicarious dancing just as there is no vicarious breathing.

By connecting the wisdom of rave celebrations to a liturgical tradition we have demonstrated that one does not need the drug Ecstasy or any other drug to "get high" or experience trance. Several ravers have commented to me that they found in our worship what they had been looking for all along in rave dances: community, deep prayer, joy and spirit, plus an additional bonus of praying with people of diverse ages. One drug counselor for youth in San Francisco took fifteen of her clients to the mass, and on the way home in the van they said to her: "This is the first time in our lives that we have gotten high without drugs." Much of the drug attraction for the young in our culture comes from their being starved for transcendent experiences in worship, in school, and at home. A Techno Cosmic Mass is one example of how imagination put to the service of a need, in this instance, community ritual, is redemptive. We need many rituals today, public and personal, to heal our souls and the souls of our various communities and to bring joy alive, truly alive. This way, creativity can flow again.

the coming dawn: the hope that creativity brings

Where does our hope lie? Where shall we ground ourselves for continuing on and changing our ways radically? Can we be confident that creativity is the key to our survival and sustainability as a species?

Creativity is who we are, creativity can redeem and save our species. I agree with Dr. Clarissa Pinkola Estés that "all women and men are born gifted." All we need to do is release this creativity, get out of its way, as M. C. Richards used to say. Estés also believes that "a woman's creative ability is her most valuable asset." I believe that is true of men as well—it is the most valuable asset of our species.

What are we waiting for? Let us remove the obstacles, let go of the guilt, and get moving. We have nothing to lose but our pessimism and cynicism, for, as Otto Rank warned us, "pessimism comes with the repression of creativity."

Creativity is not in short supply. There is an abundance of it, plenty to go around. It has always been this way. From the original fireball to the birth of the atoms, galaxies, supernovas, stars, sun, planets, earth and her marvelous creatures. We humans are latecomers to the creative universe, but we are powerfully endowed with creativity.

Some of my hope comes from the realization, growing daily, of how perilous our situation is on this planet. As more and more people get out of denial and the addictions denial puts us in and come to realize the danger that our unsustainable species is in, there will be action and there will be grounds for hope. This sounds paradoxical, and it is: Our very despair is a cause of hope, for despair often results in breakdown, and breakdown results in breakthrough. Our systems are breaking down today—all of them. And we feel it. All our professions, all our religions, all our politics and economic and educational establishments need reinventing. They all lack feminine energy, wisdom energy. They lack cosmology and creativity.

This gives hope—that the Divine can and will return in a more balanced form to our species. It will return through a coming alive of our love of life and a response to the pain so omnipresent on our planet. This response will precipitate an outbreak of creativity. If we can use justice and compassion as contours to contain and to critique the use of creativity, then what we give birth to will serve other generations and other species instead of destroy them. Then the Spirit will be at work once again, creating and re-creating, co-working with humankind.

Let us not deceive ourselves or live in a silly illusion about our creativity. *Creativity is a choice.* (In theological terms, it is grace and works operating together. It is an option to live a life with grace.) Creativity is *not* a particular gift given to certain people only. It is a personal choice and a cultural choice. An individual choice and a family, professional, and societal choice, and at this time in our history it is a species choice. We choose whether to let creativity flow or not—in our educational systems, our media, our politics, our economics, our religions, our very psyches. In theological terms, it is a matter of letting the Spirit in, the Christ in, the Buddha nature in.

I believe Sri Aurobindo had this in mind when he predicted a "coming dawn" for the resurrection of poetry itself—provided we tap into a "larger cosmic vision" that would and could release the "Divine possibilities" of our species. Perhaps Hildegard of Bingen, the twelfth-century abbess, mystic, scientist, and artist, put it best when she said:

> *God has gifted creation with everything that is necessary. . . .*
> *Humankind, full of all creative possibilities, is God's work.*
> *Humankind is called to co-create. . . .*
> *God gave to humankind the talent to create with all the world.*

Just as the person shall never end, until into dust they are
transformed and resurrected,
just so, their works are always visible.
The good deeds shall glorify, the bad deeds shall shame.

It is true that we are a species that can say "NO" to our potential. We can choose not to develop our creativity and that of our children; we can choose to turn our creativity over to others and to institutions that appear more imposing than ourselves. Yes, we can use our creativity for demonic purposes—even to deny our powers of creation is to serve demonic powers that will willingly fill the gap. Yes, we can resist evolution—even our own. And our bad deeds will shame. And our species will end, bringing down much beauty with it.

But I do believe, and I am sure the reader believes, that humankind can opt instead for the "good deeds that glorify." We must. The Spirit of Creativity is expecting us to do so. Creation is waiting for our response.

{bibliography}

Anand, Margo. *The Art of Sexual Ecstasy.* New York: Tarcher/Putnam, 1989.

Arrien, Angeles. *The Nine Muses: A Mythological Path to Creativity.* New York: Tarcher/Putnam, 2000.

Asante, Molefi Kete, and Abu S. Abarry, eds. *African Intellectual Heritage: A Book of Sources.* Philadelphia: Temple University Press, 1996.

Aurobindo, Sri. *The Future Poetry.* Pondicherry, India: Sri Aurobindo Ashram Publication, 1985.

Bachelard, Gaston. *The Poetics of Space.* Boston: Beacon Press, 1994.

Berry, Thomas. *The Great Work.* New York: Bell Tower, 1999.

Borg, Marcus J. *Meeting Jesus Again for the First Time.* San Francisco: HarperSanFrancisco, 1994.

Brueggemann, Walter. *The Prophetic Imagination.* Philadelphia: Fortress Press, 1978.

Cameron, Julia. *The Artist's Way.* New York: Tarcher/Putnam, 1992.

Ching, Kaleo, and Elise Dirlam-Ching. *Tao of Creativity, Books One and Two.* Berkeley, POB 8456, 2001.

Corbin, Henri. *Creative Imagination in the Sufism of Ibn Arabi.* Princeton, NJ: Princeton University Press, 1969.

Crossan, John Dominic. *The Essential Jesus.* San Francisco: HarperSanFrancisco, 1994.

———. *The Historical Jesus.* San Francisco: HarperSanFrancisco, 1991.

———. *Jesus: A Revolutionary Biography.* San Francisco: HarperSanFrancisco, 1994.

———. *Who Killed Jesus?* San Francisco: HarperSanFrancisco, 1995.

Diaz, Adrianna. *Feeling the Creative Spirit.* San Francisco: HarperSanFrancisco, 1992.

Doyle, Brendan. *Meditations with Julian of Norwich.* Santa Fe, NM: Bear & Co., 1983.

Emoto, Masaru. *Messages from Water.* Tokyo: HADO Kyoikusha, 2001.

Estés, Clarissa Pinkola. *Women Who Run with the Wolves.* New York: Ballantine Books, 1992.

Fox, Matthew. *The Coming of the Cosmic Christ.* San Francisco: HarperSanFrancisco, 1988.

———. *One River, Many Wells: Wisdom Springing from Global Faiths.* New York: Tarcher/Putnam, 2000.

———. *Original Blessing.* Santa Fe: Bear & Co., 1983.

————. *Passion for Creation: The Earth-Honoring Spirituality of Meister Eckhart* (formerly *Breakthrough*). Rochester, VT: Inner Traditions, 2000.

————. *The Reinvention of Work.* San Francisco: HarperSanFrancisco, 1994.

————. *Sheer Joy: Conversations with Thomas Aquinas on Creation Spirituality.* San Francisco: HarperSanFrancisco, 1992.

————. *Sins of the Spirit, Blessings of the Flesh: Lessons for Transforming Evil in Soul and Society.* New York: Harmony Books, 1999.

Fox, Matthew, and Rupert Sheldrake. *The Physics of Angels.* San Francisco: HarperSanFrancisco, 1996.

Gablik, Suzi. *The Reenchantment of Art.* New York: Thames and Hudson, 1991.

Gardner, Howard. *The Arts and Human Development.* New York: Basic Books, 1994.

————. *Creating Minds.* New York: Basic Books, 1993.

Gimbutas, Marija. *The Civilization of the Goddess.* San Francisco: HarperSanFrancisco, 1991.

Hageneder, Fred. *The Spirit of Trees: Science, Symbiosis and Inspiration.* Edinburgh: Floris Books, 2000.

Hanh, Thich Nhat. *Living Buddha, Living Christ.* New York: Riverhead, 1995.

————. *The Miracle of Mindfulness.* Boston: Beacon Press, 1975.

Harvey, Andrew. *The Direct Path.* New York: Broadway Books, 2000.

————. *Son of Man.* New York: Tarcher/Putnam, 1998.

Hobday, Jose. *Simple Living.* New York: Continuum, 1999.

Kelly, Marjorie. *The Divine Right of Capital.* San Francisco: Berrett-Koehler Publishers, 2001.

Korten, David C. *The Post-Corporate World.* San Francisco: Berrett-Koehler Publishers, 1999.

Kramer, Robert. "The Birth of Client-Centered Therapy: Carl Rogers, Otto Rank, and 'The Beyond.'" *Journal of Humanistic Psychology* 35, no. 4 (Fall 1955: 54–110).

————. *A Psychology of Difference: The American Lectures of Otto Rank.* Princeton, NJ: Princeton University Press, 1996.

Ladinsky, Daniel, trans. *The Gift: Poems by Hafiz the Great Sufi Master.* New York: Penguin, 1999.

Leon-Portilla, Miguel, ed. *Native Mesoamerican Spirituality.* New York: Paulist Press, 1980.

Lopez, Barry Holstun. *About This Life: Journeys on the Threshold of Memory.* New York: Alfred A. Knopf, 1998.

Mack, Burton L. *The Lost Gospel: The Book of Q & Christian Origins.* San Francisco: HarperSanFrancisco, 1994.

Marks, William E. *The Holy Order of Water.* Great Barrington, MA: Bell Pond Books, 2001.

Mascaro, Juan, trans. *The Upanishads.* New York: Penguin, 1965.

Matt, Daniel C. *The Essential Kabbalah.* San Francisco: HarperSanFrancisco, 1996.

Matthews, Caitlin, and John Weinberg. *The Encyclopedia of Celtic Wisdom: The Celtic Shaman's Sourcebook.* Rockport, MA: Element, 1994.

May, Rollo. *The Courage to Create.* New York: Norton, 1975.

————. *My Quest for Beauty.* Dallas: Saybrook, 1985.

Merkle, John C. *The Genesis of Faith: The Depth Theology of Abraham Joshua Heschel.* New York: Macmillan, 1985.

Ming-Dao, Deng. *Everyday Tao.* San Francisco: HarperSanFrancisco, 1996.

O'Donohue, John. *Anam Cara: A Book of Celtic Wisdom.* New York: HarperCollins, 1997.

Paladin, David. *Painting the Dream: The Visionary Art of Navajo Painter David Chethlahe Paladin.* Rochester, VT: Park Street Press, 1992.

Philbrick, Nathaniel. *In the Heart of the Sea: The Tragedy of the Whaleship Essex.* New York: Penguin, 2000.

Rank, Otto. *Art and Artist.* New York: Agathon Press, 1975.

———. *Beyond Psychology.* New York: Dover, 1958.

Richards, Dona Marimba. *Let the Circle Be Unbroken: The Implications of African Spirituality in the Diaspora.* Lawrenceville, NJ: Red Sea Press, 1992.

Richards, M. C. *Centering: In Pottery, Poetry and the Person.* Middletown, CT: Wesleyan University Press, 1962.

———. *Imagine Inventing Yellow: New and Selected Poems.* Barrington, NY: Station Hill, 1991.

Roddick, Anita. *Business As Unusual.* London: HarperCollins, 2000.

Ross, Hugh McGregor. *The Gospel of Thomas.* Longmead, Shaftsbury, Dorset: Element Books, 1991.

Russell, Peter. *The White Hole in Time.* San Francisco: HarperSanFrancisco, 1992.

Schaef, Anne Wilson. *When Society Becomes an Addict.* San Francisco: Harper & Row, 1987.

Sheehan, Thomas. *The First Coming: How the Kingdom of God Became Christianity.* New York: Random House, 1986.

Swimme, Brian. *The Heart of the Cosmos.* Maryknoll, NY: Orbis Books, 1996.

Swimme, Brian, and Thomas Berry. *The Universe Story.* SanFrancisco: HarperSanFrancisco, 1992.

Thurman, Howard. *The Creative Encounter.* Richmond, IN: Friends United Press, 1972.

————. *Deep River and the Negro Spiritual Speaks of Life and Death.* Richmond, IN: Friends United Press, 1975.

Uhlein, Gabrielle. *Meditations with Hildegard of Bingen.* Santa Fe, NM: Bear & Co., 1982.

Wolf, Aline D. *Nurturing the Spirit in Non-sectarian Classrooms.* Hollidaysburg, PA: Parent Child Press, 1996.

{ index }

{ permissions }

{ acknowledgments }

I want to thank the many authors named in the Bibliography. I especially want to thank Joel Fotinos and Mitch Horowitz of Jeremy Tarcher for their urging me to write this book and for Mitch's fine editorial suggestions. Also my agent, Ned Leavitt, for his masterly coaching and ongoing encouragement. To Allison Sobel at Tarcher and to faculty and students at the University of Creation Spirituality and Naropa University, with a special thanks to Judith Coates. Special thanks to Javier Garcia for his art and our hours of conversation on the nature of the creative process.

For more information about Matthew Fox and the degrees offered at the University of Creation Spirituality and Naropa Oakland, see www.creationspirituality.org.